Ethics
in the Workplace^{2e}

Keith Goree

Director, Applied Ethics Institute

Saint Petersburg College

Saint Petersburg, Florida

THOMSON

SOUTH-WESTERN

Australia · Brazil · Canada · Mexico · Singapore · Spain · United Kingdom · United States

THOMSON

SOUTH-WESTERN

Ethics in the Workplace, Second Edition
Keith Goree

VP/Editorial Director:
Jack W. Calhoun

VP/Editor-in-Chief:
Karen Schmohe

Executive Editor:
Eve Lewis

Developmental Editor:
Karen Hein

Consulting Editor:
Marianne Miller

Marketing Manager:
Nancy Long

Content Project Manager:
Diane Bowdler

Production Manager:
Patricia Matthews Boies

Manufacturing Coordinator:
Kevin Kluck

Production House:
Interactive Composition Corporation

Printer:
Edwards Brothers
Ann Arbor, MI

Art Director:
Tippy McIntosh

Internal Designer:
Lou Ann Thesing

Cover Designer:
Lou Ann Thesing

Cover Images:
© Paul Anderson/Images.com

Photo Researcher:
Darren Wright

For more information about our
products, contact us at:

Thomson Higher Education
5191 Natorp Boulevard
Mason, Ohio 45040
USA

Introduction to Students

A teenager returns a wallet that he found (and the money in it) to its owner. Another teen is caught cheating on an exam. A classmate volunteers several hours of her time every week to tutor elementary school children. Another girl lies on a job application. One employee in a department store figures out a way to help the environment by recycling old boxes. Another employee occasionally steals merchandise from the store. Everywhere you look it seems as though you are surrounded by ethical issues and concerns.

  In this textbook, you will explore what makes actions right or wrong, why people choose to do what is right, and how to apply those ideas to the workplace. Before you begin your study of ethics, however, there are a few important things about this book that you need to know.

Ethics in the Workplace will . . .

- Help you become more sensitive to the ethical issues in everyday life and at work. Once you learn to recognize ethical issues, you will be amazed at all of the places you see them—at home, at school, in your community, and around the world.
- Encourage you to learn to think more clearly, critically, and logically about difficult ethical issues and questions. Carefully thinking through an ethical problem is the first step in finding the best answer.
- Offer tools necessary to make more mature and responsible ethical decisions— decisions on which you can look back later with pride, rather than regret.
- Help you understand the vastly different consequences of ethical and unethical behavior at work.
- Give you an opportunity to raise your own personal ethical standards to new, higher levels. You must choose to raise these standards for yourself. This higher road is not an easy one, or more people would take it. However, as you grow in moral maturity, you will find that people treat you more as an adult and less as a child. They will respect and trust you more.
- Assist you as you set sail on what it is hoped will be a life-long search for the best answers to life's problems; the best ethical principles to live by; and eventually, a good life.

Ethics in the Workplace will not . . .

- Provide you with a list of rules and regulations to obey in life. The goal of studying ethics is to learn to make responsible and mature moral decisions on your own.
- Give you a list of opinions with which you are expected to agree. This book is about the process of making decisions about right and wrong.

- Try to manipulate or control your moral beliefs or opinions. An important part of ethical maturity is developing your own beliefs and opinions for your own reasons.
- Force you to share your private beliefs, opinions, feelings, and experiences with others. Your right to privacy will be respected.

The Organization of *Ethics in the Workplace*

The first four chapters represent the foundations of ethics. In those chapters, you will investigate the nature of ethics, as well as principles that can be used in making ethical decisions. You will learn about the process of moral development. You will also acquire critical-thinking skills that can be useful in finding answers to ethical questions.

Chapters 5 through 11 focus on specific ethical issues in the workplace. Those issues are timely and relevant in America today. In fact, you may be surprised to find how frequently you see the topics discussed in class on the front page of the newspaper and on the evening news.

Each chapter offers a thorough discussion of a specific topic relevant to business ethics. In addition, each chapter includes reinforcement activities (sometimes with a creative twist!), critical-thinking exercises, and a variety of opportunities for personal reflection and growth.

What's New in This Edition?

- *What Do You Think?* Presents an original scenario about an ethical issue or problem confronting people at work.
- *You Decide* Gives you an opportunity to thoughtfully evaluate examples of ethical and unethical behaviors.
- *Checkpoint* Provides a recurring tool for reviewing key terms.
- *Real-World Ethics* Presents current examples of what people are doing with ethics in the workplace and in society.
- *The ETHICS Model* Offers a systematic approach to analyze ethical problems and dilemmas to make the best possible decisions.
- *Ethics & Law* Highlights the legal implications of important ethical ideas.
- *Vocabulary Builder* Tests your understanding of ethical concepts.
- *Learn More* Offers guided research into specific ethical questions, issues, and concepts.
- *Digging Deeper* Suggests creative follow-up activities to see how these concepts work in the real world.

Tips for Getting the Most from This Course

- Focus on understanding new concepts and learning to apply them to ethical questions. Simply memorizing definitions won't do you much good. Keep asking yourself, What does this mean? and How can I use this?
- Stay open-minded to new ideas and different points of view. Someone said that a mind is like a parachute—it only functions properly when it is open. You cannot learn anything as long as you think you already have all of the answers.

- Keep holding yourself up to the ethical mirror. Evaluate your own ethical strengths and weaknesses as honestly as you can. If you think of this course simply as new words to be learned and blanks to be filled in, you miss the most important lessons.
- For additional information on ethics topics, see Keith Goree's articles in the online newsletter *The Balance Sheet* at www.balancesheet.swlearning.com.

Acknowledgments

I thank the following individuals who contributed to the review process for this edition:

Betty Banks-Burke
Co-Department Chair, Business Education/Computer Science
Hudson High School
Hudson, Ohio

Carol D. Cox
Business Teacher
Westwood High School
Ishpeming, Michigan

Nina J. Kyler
Director, Career Development Center
Leo High School
Leo, Indiana

Kristine Labbus
Business Education
Neenah High School
Neenah, Wisconsin

Vickie L. Banks Reed
Manager, Marketing/Verizon
Dallas/Fort Worth, Texas

Mark Steedly
Sports Marketing Instructor
Great Oaks Institute of Technology/Winton Woods High School
Cincinnati, Ohio

Mary Tidd
Business Teacher
Martinsville High School
Martinsville, Indiana

John P. Webster
Marketing, Management, & Entrepreneurship Instructor
DeForest Area High School
DeForest, Wisconsin

Keith Goree
Saint Petersburg, Florida

Contents

Chapter 11   Ethics and Corporate Responsibility

1

Welcome to Ethics!

Chapter Goals

After completing this chapter, you should be able to:

■ Explain basic ethical terms and concepts.

■ Evaluate various sources of ethical beliefs.

■ Explain what makes ethics different from other standards of behavior.

Key Terms & Concepts

ethical principles

universal (principles)

ethics

morality

ethical issues

relativism

legalism

authority

culture

intuition

reason

standard

standard of etiquette

standard of law

standard of ethics

What do you think?

It's a beautiful weekend in late spring. Instead of being out with her friends (where she would prefer to be), Tamika has been hunting for a summer job—her first job. She has scoured the want ads, walked boldly into most stores in the mall, and even checked out a couple of large department stores near her home. Not many places are willing to hire someone under 18, but she has found a few possibilities. Now she's at home with her best friend, Marilyn, filling out employment applications.

Marilyn has been through this process before and says that she knows the secret for landing any job.

"It's called padding your resume," Marilyn states with authority. "You just have to exaggerate the things you've done to make them sound more impressive. For example, sometimes you used to baby-sit the neighbor's kids after school. We'll call that 'extensive supervisory experience in child care.' And weren't you the treasurer for Junior Honor Society? Let's put down 'financial manager for a national nonprofit organization.' See, it's easy!"

Tamika is growing uncomfortable. "Marilyn, I'm intentionally misleading people to think I'm somebody I'm not. Isn't that lying? And besides, what are they going to think if I do get the job and show up as the real me? Won't they be disappointed?"

Marilyn replies, "No, it's not lying. We aren't making up things that aren't true. We're just maximizing your strengths! And you can be Miss Goody Two-Shoes if you want, but you'll be stuck at home without a job. Everyone out there is doing this. If you want to compete for a decent job, this is what you have to do!"

Tamika looks at her application. She's just written that she has "substantial experience in secondary-level educational administration." That did sound a lot better than saying she spent fifth period as a student aide in the school office. But maybe it sounded too much better. . . .

What do you think?

What do you think about Tamika's temptation? Is there anything wrong with Tamika padding her resume to make her more competitive in the job market? Granted, those examples are a bit exaggerated; but is it acceptable to be more subtle? What if you wrote that you worked somewhere for two years instead of six months or that you left a prior job with excellent evaluations when, in fact, you received poor evaluations?

Every day you make decisions about whether actions are right or wrong. But how often do you stop to think about why you believe a behavior is right or why it is wrong? In this chapter, you will investigate different answers to that question and begin to discover what ethics is about.

You Decide

1. If you found a wallet containing $50, would it be wrong to keep the money? Why or why not?

_____

_____

2. If you could win at a sport more often by cheating occasionally, would it be wrong to cheat? Why or why not?

_____

_____

3. If a friend got an unflattering haircut, would it be wrong to lie and tell the person that it looked good? Why or why not?

_____

_____

4. If you dropped your parent's business cell phone, which you were *not* supposed to be using, while calling a friend, would it be wrong to lie about how the phone was broken? Why or why not?

_____

_____

5. If you found out that a classmate was selling illegal drugs, would it be wrong to keep quiet about what you learned? Why or why not?

_____

_____

That exercise provides several clues to help you understand ethics. First, many areas of life contain questions concerning right and wrong. People face ethical decisions at home, at school, at work, in their friendships and romances, and sometimes when they're all alone.

Second, people's ethical beliefs are unique. People base ethical decisions on their personal values and principles, which are developed through individual life experiences. Since everyone has different experiences, it seems reasonable that principles, values, and decisions will vary, too.

Third, notice that your answers included two parts. Each part can tell you something about your ethics. In your yes/no response, you expressed your ethical opinions. Making decisions like those is an important part of the ethical process. However, the most important part of ethics has to do with your *why* response, in which you likely referred to some of your ethical principles.

Ethical principles are general statements of how people *should* or *should not* act. Principles are often the reasons behind a person's actions, thoughts, and beliefs. Those principles are often described as **universal**, meaning that rational people thinking logically would have to agree that everyone should follow them. A popular universal ethical principle is known as the Golden Rule—you should treat others as you would want to be treated. Other common principles include the following:

- People should respect the rights of others.
- People should keep their promises.
- People should be honest.
- People should take responsibility for their actions.
- People should act in the best interests of others.
- People should help others in need when possible.
- People should be fair.

"The world has achieved brilliance without conscience. Ours is a world of nuclear giants and ethical infants."

—General Omar Bradley

Personal Reflection

Look at your answers to "You Decide" and consider the following questions.

1. In which part of your life do you face the most ethical problems and decisions? Why do you think that is?

2. What do your answers say about the kind of person you are?

3. How many of your classmates do you think answered the questions the same way you did?

4. What major life experiences have affected your personal ethics the most?

5. What ethical principle(s) do you see behind the responses you gave? (Remember, the principles are in the *why* part of your answer.)

• Question 1:

• Question 2:

• Question 3:

• Question 4:

• Question 5:

Do you see how one moral decision can have several ethical principles behind it? Understanding principles like those—and learning to apply them to different ethical situations and issues—is at the heart of understanding what ethics is about.

What Is Ethics All About?

Ethical terms often mean different things to different people. Some individuals even claim that ethical terms have no valid meanings at all. In this section, you will be introduced to several foundational definitions. You also will analyze arguments against the existence of moral right and wrong.

The Language of Ethics

Ethics is the subfield of philosophy that studies the morality of human conduct, that is, what is considered right or wrong, good or bad. **Morality** refers to that part of human behavior that can be evaluated in terms of right and wrong. Technically speaking, then, ethics is the study of morality. However, in practical usage, the words *ethical* and *moral* are used to describe actions that are considered to be good or right, while the words *unethical* and *immoral* are used to describe actions that are considered to be bad or wrong.

Ethical issues are topics or actions that raise questions of right and wrong. Examples include stealing, cheating, lying, and driving drunk. But those behaviors don't raise very difficult questions, do they? If they are honest with themselves, even thieves, cheaters, liars, and drunk drivers know that their actions are wrong.

Other ethical issues are more difficult and require more thought and analysis. Some people argue that everything on the Internet, including commercially recorded music, movies, and television shows, should be available free for anyone who wants to download them. That idealistic view of a free and open exchange of art sounds wonderful until you put yourself in the shoes of the artists who created the works. Why would people invest millions of dollars creating music or films if they knew that they would never get their money back, much less make a profit? While it sounds nice on the surface, a policy of "free art for all" might actually mean the end of quality works of music and film that so many people enjoy.

Do Right and Wrong Exist?

Do the concepts of moral right and wrong really exist? Some people argue that the ideas have been social inventions to control people's behavior. That point of view asserts that right and wrong are little more than emotional reactions, religious assumptions, or social agreements. That skepticism is often based on two arguments.

The first is **relativism**, the belief that because ethical beliefs vary so widely, there can be no universal ethical principles that apply to everyone. After all, no two individuals, societies, or religions agree completely on what is right or wrong. If a set of moral guidelines did exist for all people, wouldn't it seem logical that everyone could agree on what those guidelines are? Since everyone does not agree, the argument continues that moral right and wrong cannot be anything more than personal opinion.

The problem with that criticism of ethics is that people *do* agree, at least most of the time. That may not seem to be the case, since people tend to focus more on their differences than their similarities. However, if you really think about it, how many people would argue that robbing and assaulting people are morally right? Even the people who do those things know they shouldn't. Or how many people believe that helping others or standing up for the truth in a difficult situation is wrong? The truth is that most people agree about the vast majority of life's ethical questions. However, it is the ethical questions that people disagree about that seem to get the most press.

The second criticism of ethics is legalism. **Legalism** is the belief that because there are laws and policies to cover issues of right and wrong, ethics is irrelevant. It's not necessary to discuss whether people should be allowed to smoke marijuana because doing so is illegal. If an action is illegal, it must be wrong. And if someone isn't sure whether an action is right or wrong, all he or she has to do is find out what the law says.

You may already understand that this problem is based on a fundamental misunderstanding about law and ethics. Yes, societies write laws to back up and formalize their ethical values and beliefs; but the laws don't take the place of those beliefs. They only reinforce them. And at times, the laws don't even do that. Sometimes societies discover that their laws are actually in conflict with their ethical values. That's what happened when Americans decided that laws allowing slavery, the second-class status of women, harmful child labor practices, and discrimination of all kinds had to be changed. *Legal* is not the same as *ethical*. In fact, the ethical standard is higher, as you will see later in this chapter.

Learn More

Use an Internet search engine to find Dr. King's "Letter from the Birmingham Jail." Record your reactions and discuss them in class.

Real-World Ethics

In 1963, Martin Luther King, Jr., went to Birmingham, Alabama, to make a speech on civil rights. In an attempt to prevent him from making that speech, city leaders announced that anyone making a public speech would have to get a special permit from city hall. Dr. King's request for a permit was denied. But Dr. King decided that such permit laws violated people's basic human (and constitutional) right to freedom of speech. He made his speech anyway and, consequently, was arrested.

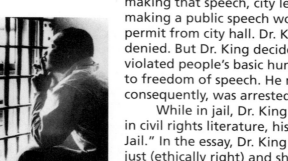
©Bettmann/CORBIS

While in jail, Dr. King wrote one of the greatest essays in civil rights literature, his "Letter from the Birmingham Jail." In the essay, Dr. King pointed out that many laws are just (ethically right) and should be obeyed by everyone. But laws can also be unjust (ethically wrong). Unjust laws must be disobeyed. So what makes a law unjust?

- Laws are unjust when they are not consistent with universal ethical principles.
- Laws are unjust when they degrade people.
- Laws are unjust when they are imposed on minority groups but are not intended to apply to everyone.
- Laws are unjust when they are imposed on groups that are not allowed to vote or are not allowed to have a voice in laws they are required to follow.
- Sometimes just laws can be used in unjust ways.

What do you think about Dr. King's explanation of unjust laws? What are some examples of laws in American history that would qualify as unjust?

Checkpoint

Define the following terms in your own words.

ethics _____

_____

morality _____

_____

ethical issues _____

_____

universal ethical principles _____

_____

relativism _____

_____

legalism _____

_____

What do you think now?

Take another look at Tamika's situation at the beginning of the chapter. Use the table below to list three ethical issues and three ethical principles to which the scenario refers. (You may have to read between the lines in the scenario.)

Ethical Issues	1. _____
	_____
	_____
	2. _____
	_____
	_____
	3. _____
	_____
	_____
Ethical Principles	1. _____
	_____
	_____
	2. _____
	_____
	_____
	3. _____
	_____
	_____

Personal Reflection

1. List two important ethical issues that you see society or your community wrestling with and debating.

   Ethical Issue 1:

   - Personal Ethical Judgment (Do you think the action in question is right or wrong?)

   - Ethical Principle (What makes it right or wrong?)

   Ethical Issue 2:

   - Personal Ethical Judgment (Do you think the action in question is right or wrong?)

   - Ethical Principle (What makes it right or wrong?)

"Not life, but a good life is to be chiefly valued."

—Socrates

2. How would you respond to the following skeptical claims about ethics? Circle *agree* or *disagree;* then explain your answer.

   a. People cannot agree about what actions are right and what actions are wrong.

      agree   **disagree**

      Why?

   b. Unless everyone agrees completely on what actions are right and what actions are wrong, the concepts of right and wrong cannot exist.

      agree   **disagree**

      Why?

   c. Because ethical decisions are based on individual beliefs, no one can judge anyone else's actions as being right or wrong.

      agree   **disagree**

      Why?

   d. Ethics are not necessary because laws prescribe what is right and what is wrong.

      agree   **disagree**

      Why?

The following facts should not come as much of a surprise.

- Everyone has ethical beliefs.
- Not everyone has the same beliefs.
- Everyone gets his or her ethical beliefs from somewhere.
- Not everyone gets his or her ethical beliefs from the same source.

However, you might be surprised to learn that there are not an infinite number of sources of ethical beliefs from which to choose. In fact, the philosopher Richard Doss has narrowed down the sources to just a few.

Sources of Ethical Beliefs

Since it seems reasonable to assume that moral right and wrong do exist in some form, where do people get the ethical principles and values that support their beliefs? Some principles are the result of lessons taught at home, in school, or in religious training. Other principles are the result of individual life experiences. For instance, children who grow up in violent neighborhoods may have different principles and beliefs than children who grow up sheltered from those dangers. Some people acquire their principles from messages that society sends through television, music, magazines, and books. In other words, people's principles come from a variety of sources. However, writer and philosopher Richard Doss has pointed out that some sources are more influential than others. When asked where they acquire their beliefs about an ethical issue, most people tend to identify one or more of the following sources. (See Illustration 1-1.)

Illustration 1-1

Authority

One source of ethical beliefs is **authority**. According to this approach, an action is right or wrong because "someone important said so." This way of thinking is often seen in religious ethics, but other moral authorities in history have included political leaders (for example, monarchs). When people say, "Stealing is morally wrong because God forbids it" or "Stealing is wrong because the government has made it illegal," they are relying on authority.

Culture

Another source of ethical beliefs is **culture**, the idea that the morality of an action depends on the beliefs of one's culture or nation. This approach says that cultures and nations, like individuals, have different values and principles based on their different experiences in history. A belief that works well for one culture may be harmful for another. Because this view assumes that there are no *universal* moral principles (remember relativism?), one logical conclusion would be that no nation or culture is able to judge the moral beliefs or actions of another nation or culture. Another conclusion might be that individuals of one culture cannot rise to a higher level of ethical thinking and living than people of another culture. And if that is true, how do cultures and societies ever improve?

Intuition

A third source of ethical beliefs is **intuition**, which is the idea that principles of right and wrong have been built into a person's conscience and that he or she will know what is right by listening to that "little voice" within. This reliance on intuition is very common. People often seem to know instinctively whether actions are right or wrong. But have you noticed how some people's ethical intuitions seem to be confused? Have you ever known someone who was blatantly prejudiced against others because of their skin color, their religion, or their homeland? Some people just don't understand. Things that are obviously wrong to everyone else don't seem wrong to them.

Reason

The fourth source of ethical beliefs is **reason**, the idea that consistent, logical thinking should be the primary tool used in making ethical decisions. According to this approach, if stealing is judged to be wrong, then there should be solid arguments and logical principles that back up that judgment. In other words, the arguments against stealing are stronger than the arguments for stealing. With the appeal to reason, an action is not wrong *just* because an authority says so, *just* because it is unpopular within a culture, or *just* because someone's inner voice warns against it. Instead, this approach suggests that a person look open-mindedly at the arguments on both sides of an issue, then use reason to carefully choose the stronger arguments.

Checkpoint

In your own words, summarize the following meanings of the sources of ethical beliefs.

authority: _____

_____

culture: _____

_____

intuition: _____

_____

reason: _____

_____

What do you think now?

Apply what you've learned about the sources of ethical beliefs to Tamika's situation at the beginning of the chapter. How would Tamika's thinking about exaggerating accomplishments on her resume vary depending on what source she was relying on? How might her decision about padding her resume be affected? Use the table below to record your answers.

Source	What Would Tamika Be Thinking?	What Would Tamika Do?
Authority		
Culture		
Intuition		
Reason		

Personal Reflection

1. Which of the sources of ethical beliefs has influenced you the most? Why?

2. Which of the sources has influenced you the least? Why?

3. Write one specific action you could take to make reasoning more of a factor in your ethical decision making.

"If a man will begin with certainties, he shall end in doubts; but if he will be content to begin with doubts, he shall end in certainties."

—Sir Francis Bacon

If you lived alone on an island somewhere, the only ethical code you would be concerned about would be your own. But life doesn't work that way. The truth is that life is more or less a group project. You experience life through your family members, friends, neighborhood, school, city, culture, and country. Therefore, you must concern yourself with the effects of your actions on others and the effects of their actions on you. You can't think about ethics only in individual terms. You are forced to consider standards that may apply to everyone.

Standards of Behavior

A **standard** is an accepted level of behavior to which people are expected to conform. The level may be set low (a minimum standard), in the middle (an average standard), or very high (a standard of excellence). Whatever the level, all standards involve some kind of expectation. To say that stealing is wrong does not mean that it is wrong for just one person or even for a few people. If stealing is forbidden by a social standard, then the assumption is that stealing is wrong for everyone. Certainly, there are ethical issues that are individual and personal, too; but ethics often deals with principles that apply to everyone. People's actions can be evaluated according to many standards; but three of the most common standards are those of etiquette, law, and ethics.

Etiquette

The **standard of etiquette** refers to expectations concerning manners or social graces. Societies and cultures have their own rules of etiquette that their members are expected to meet. Most people understand their social etiquette standards and try to live up to them. Thus, a person knows to knock before entering someone else's home and tries to remember to say "please" and "thank you." It is assumed that everyone understands these rules, even though many of them are not written down. (Oddly enough, almost everyone knows exactly how loud a burp can be before it is considered rude.) People who violate the standards of etiquette run the risk of being embarrassed or of having others look down on them. Some large corporations actually send their employees to etiquette classes. Proper manners are that important to the company image!

In a crowded, busy, and stressed society, etiquette also reduces social friction and makes it easier for people to live together as a community. But there is an important difference between the standards of etiquette and ethics; that difference is *seriousness*. The issues covered by the standard of etiquette are not as serious as those that pertain to ethics. People rarely die due to poor manners; but the ethical standard applies to many life-and-death issues such as abortion, euthanasia, war, capital punishment, and AIDS. Even ethical issues that are not associated with death, such as censorship, honesty in government, and sexual ethics, still have serious implications.

Law

The **standard of law** has to do with rules of behavior imposed on people by governments. Like ethics, this legal standard can be serious, too. After all, many laws deal with life-and-death issues, including rules forbidding murder, drunken driving, drug use, and child abuse. Yet while legal and ethical standards are serious, there is an important difference—*validity*. What makes a law valid (or what gives it legal force) is different from what makes an ethical principle or judgment valid.

Have you ever wondered what makes a law valid? Let's use critical thinking skills to find that answer together.

Assume that the speed limit in front of your house is 25 miles per hour. What might make that law valid? Remember, you aren't looking at just this one law. You want to discover the factor that makes all laws valid.

Speed Limit: Possible Validating Factors	Works With This Law?	True for All Laws?
It's posted on a sign.	No, you could change the number on the sign—but don't; that's called vandalism.	No, laws can be valid even when most people don't know about them.
It's enforced by police.	No, 25 mph would be the speed limit even if the police didn't enforce it.	No, laws can be valid even when they aren't enforced.
Everyone obeys it.	Everyone obeys the speed limit? Since when?	No, laws remain valid even when people break them.
People voted for it.	No one gets to vote for speed limits.	No, laws can be valid without anyone voting for them.
It's morally right.	Driving safely may be a moral duty; going 25 mph doesn't seem as clear-cut.	No, laws can be valid even when they are morally wrong (slavery, for example).
It makes sense.	Tough call. 25 mph on a neighborhood street might make sense.	No, or there couldn't be valid laws that don't make sense—and there are. (See "Ethics & Law.")
It was instituted by a legitimate authority.	Bingo! 25 mph is the law because the local government employees who posted that speed limit had the legitimate authority to do so.	Bingo! The only factor that makes a law valid is authority. If the legitimate authority says the 25 mph speed limit is a law, it's a law.

Learn More

Use the Internet to find more examples of "dumb laws." Bring one or two to class to share. Remember, the point is that laws don't have to make sense to be considered valid.

Ethics & Law

Can laws be valid if they don't seem to make any logical sense? Consider these examples of laws that are (or were) valid.

- Lawrence, KS   It is illegal to walk through town with bees in your hat.
- Brooklyn, NY   It is illegal to allow a donkey to sleep in your bathtub.
- Augusta, GA   It is against the law to steal other people's garbage.
- Andover, MD   The use of "space guns" is legally forbidden.
- Iowa   A kiss lasting more than five minutes is illegal.
- Louisiana   It is illegal to hunt lizards at night.
- Massachusetts   Dueling with water pistols is against the law.
- Helsinki, Finland   Instead of giving parking tickets, police may deflate tires.
- Florida   It is illegal to bathe in your bathtub naked.

> "Man is the only animal that blushes, or needs to."
>
> —Mark Twain

Ethics

So the only factor that matters in determining the validity of a law is whether the person who proclaimed the law had the legitimate authority to do so. With the ethical standard, however, authority is not what matters. The **standard of ethics** refers to social expectations of people's *moral* behavior. The ethical principles and rules making up this standard are made valid by *the reasons and arguments supporting them.* If you stated, "The death penalty is morally wrong," what you're really saying is that the reasons and arguments supporting that statement make more logical sense than the reasons and arguments on the other side of the debate. Authority is not the issue. For ethical statements to be valid, they must make logical sense.

Because of that crucial difference, legal standards and moral standards do not always agree. As a result, actions can be described in four ways:

- Legally and morally right
- Legally wrong but morally right
- Legally right but morally wrong
- Legally and morally wrong

As a result, people sometimes have to choose between obeying the law and doing what they believe is morally right. Many people in history have gone to prison—and even to their deaths—rather than violate their ethical beliefs and principles.

Another difference between legal and ethical standards is that legal standards (based on authority) may change as authorities change, but ethical standards (based on reason) change only when new information causes people's thinking about the standards to change. Also, a legal standard discourages people from questioning and challenging it, since those actions are often perceived as threats to authority. On the other hand, an ethical standard *requires* the honest questioning and challenging that comes with independent thinking, for that is the only way a society can continue to learn and find better answers.

Checkpoint

1. How is the standard of ethics different from the standard of etiquette?

_____

_____

2. What is the difference between the standard of ethics and the standard of law?

_____

_____

What do you think now?

Consider Tamika's situation at the beginning of the chapter. Assume that she is applying for a job that requires her to swear under oath that everything on her resume is true. Lying on the application would represent perjury, a crime. Apply what you've learned about the differences between the legal standard and the ethical standard. Record your answers in the table below.

Statement	What Makes This Statement Valid?
Exaggerating your accomplishments on this resume is legally wrong.	
Exaggerating your accomplishments on this resume is ethically wrong.	

Personal Reflection

1. Give an example of a situation in which the standard of etiquette turned out to be important to you.

2. Describe a situation when you were confronted with the importance (and potential consequences) of the legal standard.

3. Provide an example of a time when you had to make a difficult ethical decision. How did the concept of the ethical standard apply to your situation?

Summary

Ethics is the study of the morality of human conduct—what is considered right or wrong, good or bad. Morality refers to human behavior that can be evaluated in terms of right and wrong. Ethical issues are topics that raise moral concerns. Ethical principles are the general guidelines by which people should live.

People tend to base their ethical beliefs on some combination of the following sources: authority, culture, intuition and reason.

The standard of ethics tends to be more serious in nature than the standard of etiquette. While the standard of law can also be quite serious, it is based on authority. In contrast, the standard of ethics is based on reason and logical thinking.

Chapter 1 Assessments

Vocabulary Builder

Match the following terms to their definitions.

1. _____ A source of ethical beliefs holding that right and wrong have been built into a person's conscience and that he or she will know what is right by listening to that "little voice" within.
2. _____ A source of ethical beliefs holding that an action is right or wrong because "someone important said so."
3. _____ The belief that because there are laws and policies to cover issues of right and wrong, ethics is irrelevant.
4. _____ The belief that because ethical beliefs vary so widely, there can be no universal ethical principles that apply to everyone.
5. _____ General guidelines of ethical behavior (of how people should act).
6. _____ The part of human conduct that can be evaluated in terms of right and wrong.
7. _____ The source of ethical beliefs holding that consistent, logical thinking should be the primary tool used in making ethical decisions.
8. _____ The source of ethical beliefs holding that the morality of an action depends on the beliefs of one's culture or nation.
9. _____ Rational people thinking logically agreeing that everyone should follow these.
10. _____ Rules of behavior imposed on people by governments.
11. _____ Social expectations concerning manners or social graces.
12. _____ Social expectations of people's moral behavior.
13. _____ The study of what is right and wrong, good and bad.
14. _____ Topics or actions that raise questions of right or wrong.
15. _____ An accepted level of behavior to which people are expected to conform.

a. ethical principles
b. universal principles
c. ethics
d. morality
e. ethical issues
f. relativism
g. legalism
h. authority
i. culture
j. intuition
k. reason
l. standard
m. standard of etiquette
n. standard of law
o. standard of ethics

Reinforcement

1. What are the two key criticisms of ethics discussed in this chapter?

_____

_____

_____

_____

2. What are the four possible sources of ethical beliefs?

_____

_____

_____

_____

3. What is the primary difference between the standards of etiquette and ethics?

_____

_____

_____

_____

4. What is the primary difference between the legal standard and the ethical standard?

_____

_____

_____

_____

Thinking Critically

Mike works part-time helping to take care of an elderly neighbor, Mr. Chura, who suffers from early-stage Alzheimer's disease. Mike buys Mr. Chura's groceries, drives him to appointments, and sometimes cooks and cleans. The disease has progressed to the point that Mr. Chura is becoming forgetful. One of Mike's friends points out how easy it would be for Mike to score some extra cash. After all, Mike knows where Mr. Chura keeps his cash, a large coin collection, and other valuables. The elderly man wouldn't be likely to notice a few missing items.

1. What is the main ethical issue involved in this story?

_____

_____

_____

_____

_____

2. How is the standard of law relevant to Mike's scenario?

_____

_____

_____

_____

_____

_____

3. How does the standard of ethics apply?

_____

_____

_____

_____

_____

_____

4. What does Mike think about his temptation if authority is his chief source of ethical beliefs?

_____

_____

_____

_____

_____

_____

5. How does Mike think differently if his main source of ethical beliefs is culture?

_____

_____

_____

_____

_____

_____

6. What if Mike relies largely on intuition?

_____

_____

_____

_____

_____

_____

7. How are Mike's actions affected if he uses reason to determine the right course of action?

_____

_____

_____

_____

_____

_____

8. List three ethical principles that Mike might consider when he is reasoning about what he should do.

_____

_____

_____

_____

_____

_____

Digging Deeper

1. Use a variety of media sources to find stories about ethical issues. Your sources can include the Internet, newspaper and magazine articles, even advertisements. Combine the stories you find with those of a classmate to create a collage about ethics.

2. List several movies or television shows in which characters violate a law in order to do what they believe is ethically or morally right. Be prepared to share your examples with the class.

Personal Reflection

Personal Reflections are reserved for your personal experiences, beliefs, and reflections. You will not be expected or required to turn in your responses.

1. List three ethical principles and rules you have adopted for your life. Where did you learn them? Who taught them to you?

   Principle/Rule 1:
   - Where did you learn it?
   - Who taught it to you?

   Principle/Rule 2:
   - Where did you learn it?
   - Who taught it to you?

   Principle/Rule 3:
   - Where did you learn it?
   - Who taught it to you?

2. Recall times when you faced ethical problems and based your decisions on one or more of the following sources of ethical beliefs: authority, culture, intuition, and reason. Give an example of a situation where you relied on each source.

   - Authority:
   - Culture:
   - Intuition:
   - Reason:

3. The most important ideas that I learned in this chapter were

4. Something that this chapter made me think about was

5. Some ideas that I would like to find out more about are

2

Ethical Principles

After completing this chapter, you should be able to:

■ Evaluate the role of consequences in ethical decision making.

■ Explain the concept of human rights.

■ Define and explain moral duties.

■ Explain the concept of moral virtues.

Key Terms & Concepts

value system	principle of rights	respect for persons
consequences	duty	virtue
egoism principle	principle of duties	principle of virtues
utility principle	universality	Golden Mean
right		

Joelle, a high school senior, is planning a career as a chemical engineer. She has a well-paying afternoon and weekend job at a local chemical plant. Joelle's supervisors are impressed with her work and have said that they plan to offer her a position as a chemical engineer as soon as she completes her college education. They have even set up a scholarship fund to help pay for some of her college expenses.

One day while checking on supplies in the warehouse, Joelle noticed four workers loading a dozen old, rusty barrels onto a flatbed truck. The barrels were labeled "HAZARDOUS" and "DANGER." Several of them appeared to be leaking. The workers said that they didn't know what was in the barrels, but had been ordered to take them to the dump.

Later, Joelle asked her boss, Mr. Espinal, for more details. Looking a little uncomfortable, Mr. Espinal told Joelle that this was a company secret. Mr. Espinal made Joelle promise not to tell anyone. He then explained that the company saved thousands of dollars a year by dumping some of its chemical waste in a lake at a nearby abandoned rock quarry, rather than paying for proper disposal. Joelle felt very uncomfortable upon learning this news. She knew that children rode their bikes in the hills around the quarry and that the city's water reservoir was only a couple of miles from the quarry.

When Joelle mentioned her concerns, Mr. Espinal reacted angrily. He told Joelle that the money saved through using "the dump" allowed the company to hire high school students for part-time jobs. He also made it clear that the company wouldn't be interested in hiring any chemical engineers who couldn't keep company secrets.

Joelle's mother is an editor at the city newspaper. Should Joelle mention "the dump" to her mother?

What do you think?

> "He cannot long be good that knows not why he is good."
>
> —Richard Carew

Not all people look at ethical issues and questions the same way. While that statement is true about most societies, diversity is especially obvious in the cultural melting pot of America. People living in the United States belong to many different subcultures, distinguished by factors such as race, culture, national origin, and religious affiliation. Each subculture can have its own unique **value system**, meaning its own way of viewing ethical right and wrong. In addition, a person's ethical beliefs are affected by his or her experiences in life, his or her peer groups, and other factors that are not yet understood. It's almost a wonder that people agree on anything at all! But sometimes they do. There are some ethical answers on which most people agree because humans share many common ethical principles. In this chapter, you will investigate some of those universal principles.

You Decide

1. Can there ever be a situation in which telling a lie is the right thing to do? Explain your answer, providing one example.

_____

_____

_____

_____

2. Is it ever ethically right to betray a friend's confidence by telling a secret that you were expected to keep? Explain your answer, providing one example.

_____

_____

_____

3. Can it ever be ethically right to use another person in such a way that he or she is harmed for your own benefit? Explain your answer, providing one example.

_____

_____

_____

_____

Personal Reflection

1. Three of my strengths as an ethical person are

2. One area of weakness that I see in myself as an ethical person is

3. Write the name of one person whom you truly respect as an ethical person and whom you wish you were more like. What qualities about that person do you most admire?

"Self-interest is but the survival of the animal in us. Humanity only begins for man with self-surrender."

—Henri Amiel

Basing Morality on Consequences

One of the most common ways of considering morality is to think of actions as having good or bad consequences. **Consequences** are the effects or results of what people do. (See Illustration 2-1.) According to this way of looking at ethics, a moral action is one that brings about good consequences and an immoral action is one that causes bad consequences. Thus, killing another person is usually considered wrong because it leads to bad consequences. Families and friends are

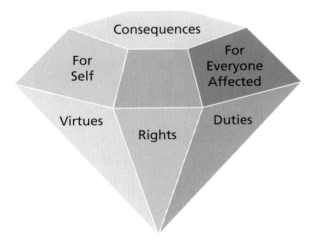

Principles for making ethical decisions

Illustration 2-1

left devastated and grieving. However, people who see ethics from the consequential perspective might argue that if the killing of another person had good results, it would be the right thing to do. Consider, for example, a scenario where a police officer has to kill one armed criminal to save the lives of many hostages. Do the officer's ends (intentions) justify his or her means (the shooting)? Most people would probably think so. Two main ethical principles, discussed next, are part of consequential ethics.

The Egoism Principle

The first principle states that you should consider only the effects an action will have on yourself and your interests. The **egoism principle** is the idea that the right thing for a person to do in any situation is the action that best serves that person's own long-term interests. (See Illustration 2-2.) No one else's interests need be considered. If you are trying to decide whether to steal money from the cash register where you work, the egoism principle would lead you to think about the effects the act would have on you. Would it be better for you in the long run to steal the money or to leave it in the register? The answer probably depends on how badly you need the money and what you think your chances are of getting caught. But according to the egoism principle, you do not need to consider the consequences for the store owner, your coworkers, or the customers. The egoism principle maintains that your only moral obligations are to yourself.

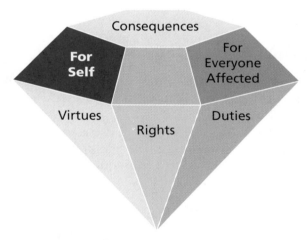

Principles for making ethical decisions

Illustration 2-2

"The greatest happiness of the greatest number is the foundation of morals and legislation."

—Jeremy Bentham

The Utility Principle

The second principle, the **utility principle**, is the idea that the morally right action is the action that produces the best consequences for everyone involved, not just for one individual. (See Illustration 2-3.) Think back to your decision about stealing the money. Using the utility principle requires that you consider the effects your action would have on everyone: you, the store owner, your coworkers, the customers, and possibly even your lawyer. In this situation, if stealing produces more *total* good or happiness for everyone than not stealing, then taking the money would be the right thing to do. If not, you should leave it in the drawer.

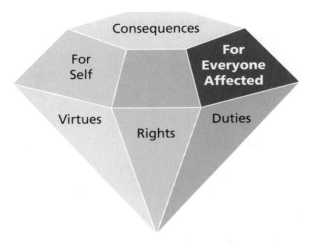

Principles for making ethical decisions

Illustration 2-3

Strengths and Weaknesses of Consequential Ethics

The strengths of these consequential approaches to ethics are that they are fairly easy to use and they seem very natural to people. After all, it is certainly wise to consider the consequences of an action before deciding whether or not to do it. However, these approaches have some serious weaknesses, too.

First, both principles require you to accurately predict the consequences of your actions. Can you really do that? The consequences of your actions often surprise you. Second, neither approach considers any action to be always right or always wrong. Killing an innocent person can be justified by the egoism principle when doing so is in a person's long-term best interests. Killing an innocent person can be permitted by the utility principle when doing so produces enough total happiness for everyone. Third, both approaches allow people to exploit or harm individuals for their own benefit (egoism) or for the benefit of the larger group (utility).

Although considering the consequences of your actions is clearly a good idea, making sound moral decisions requires more than that.

Checkpoint

1. In your own words, explain the meanings of the egoism and utility principles.

a. egoism principle: _____

_____

b. utility principle: _____

_____

2. List several strengths and weaknesses of relying solely on the principles of consequential ethics when making ethical decisions. Use the textbook to get started, but try to think of other examples.

a. strengths: _____

_____

b. weaknesses: _____

_____

What do you think now?

1. If Joelle based her decision on the principle of egoism, how would she make her decisions? What action seems to be in Joelle's best long-term interest? Why?

_____

_____

2. If Joelle based her decision on the principle of utility, how would she make her decision? What action would have the best overall consequences for everyone? Why?

_____

_____

Personal Reflection

1. Write about a recent experience when you had a difficult decision to make and thought carefully about the consequences (to yourself or others) to help you make a wise decision.

2. Write about a personal experience in which the consequences of a decision you had to make did not turn out the way you expected.

3. Write about a decision you made in which an individual's interests were harmed in some way—either for your benefit or for a larger group's benefit. Looking back on your decision, do you think you made the right choice? Why or why not?

Basing Morality on Individual Rights

A third way of considering ethics involves basing moral decisions on individual rights. A **right** refers to how an individual is entitled to be treated by others. (See Illustration 2-4.) For example, your *right to life* implies that others should not take away your life because they owe you the opportunity to live. Your *right to property* implies that others should not steal your material possessions. The Declaration of Independence and the Constitution of the United States specifically refer to many such rights, including life, liberty, the pursuit of happiness, free speech, and a fair trial. In more recent years, society has debated whether individuals have the right to die with dignity; the right to have access to quality, affordable health care; the right to have an abortion; and the right to smoke cigarettes in public places.

Learn More

The Magna Carta (1215), the U.S. Declaration of Independence (1776), and the United Nations' Universal Declaration of Human Rights (1948) are among the most important documents in history dealing with human rights. Use the Internet to find the text of these documents. Note what they have to say about individual rights and freedoms. Bring one example to class for discussion.

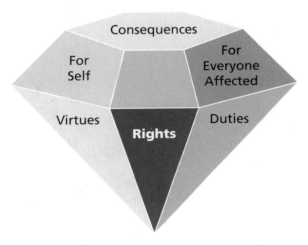

Principles for making ethical decisions

Illustration 2-4

The Principle of Rights

According to the **principle of rights**, an action is considered moral when it respects the rights of others and is considered immoral when it violates another's rights. Therefore, stealing from the cash register would be considered wrong because in taking other people's money, you are violating their property rights. Good or bad consequences are not what make an action right or wrong. Stealing from someone would nearly always violate that person's rights, even if the consequences of the theft were good for you or for a larger group.

Strengths and Weaknesses of the Principle of Rights

A strength of the principle of rights is that it gives people a great deal of moral freedom. As long as you don't violate the rights of others, you can do whatever you want. This emphasis on independence and personal freedom is probably why the founders of the United States made rights such an important part of the government and the legal system. However, the rights approach has drawbacks, too. One is that people do not always agree on what their rights are. Your fifteen-year-old friend may think he has the right to stay out all night, but his parents probably disagree. If it were easy to sort out what rights people have, debates over issues such as abortion, the death penalty, and euthanasia would have been settled long ago.

Checkpoint

1. Define the principle of rights.

_____

_____

_____

2. List several examples of your rights.

_____

_____

_____

3. List one strength and one weakness of relying only on the principle of rights when making ethical decisions.

_____

_____

_____

What do you think now?

If Joelle based her decision on individual rights, what would she think about in making her decision? Whose rights are involved in this case? Why?

_____

_____

_____

_____

_____

_____

Personal Reflection

List five individual rights that are especially important to you. Explain why you feel that way about them.

a.

b.

c.

d.

e.

Basing Morality on Duties

Another approach to considering ethics focuses on moral duties. A moral **duty** is an ethical obligation that one individual has to others. (See Illustration 2-5.) Notice that this definition is the opposite of the one given for a right. In fact, rights and duties can be thought of as opposite sides of the same coin. Your right to life implies that others have a moral duty not to kill you. Your neighbor's right to privacy implies that you have a duty not to read her mail without her permission. Other universal moral duties include obligations to help those in need, to tell the truth, and to provide for your children or aging parents.

"Everyone is really responsible to all men and for everything."

—Fyodor Dostoyevski

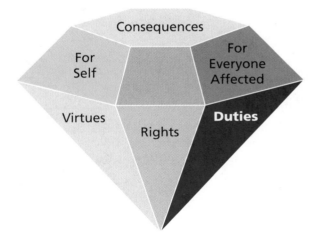

Principles for making ethical decisions

Illustration 2-5

The Principle of Duties

The **principle of duties** maintains that you should do what is ethically right purely because you have a moral obligation to do what is ethically right. Do the right thing because it's the right thing to do.

One of the classic explanations of ethical duties came from the German philosopher Immanuel Kant (1724–1804). He wrote that fulfilling moral duties is the very heart of ethics. A person's primary moral duty is to base his or her actions on good reasoning. Kant believed that good reasoning will lead all people to accept two main ethical principles, universality and respect for persons. The concept of **universality** is the idea that you should act as you would want others to act in the same situation. According to the concept of **respect for persons**, it is always wrong to use other people in ways that harm them for your own benefit. In other words, it is wrong to take unfair advantage of others for personal gain.

Strengths and Weaknesses of the Principle of Duties

A strength of basing ethics on duties is that this principle motivates people to the highest levels of ethical behavior. Concepts such as universality and respect for persons are extremely challenging to live up to. On the other hand, people do not seem to agree with one another about what their moral duties are. Some people might think that every individual has a moral duty to serve in the military. Does the fact that they think so make it an actual duty of yours? How could a society agree on what people's moral duties should be?

Checkpoint

1. Define the principle of duties.

_____

_____

2. Explain these concepts:

a. universality: _____

_____

b. respect for persons: _____

_____

3. List one strength and one weakness of relying only on the principle of duties when making ethical decisions.

_____

_____

_____

What do you think now?

If Joelle based her decision on moral duties, what would she think about in making her decision? What moral duties do you think she should consider? How would the principles of universality and respect for persons apply?

_____

_____

_____

_____

_____

_____

_____

_____

Personal Reflection

List five moral or ethical duties that are important in your life. Remember, these are obligations that you have to others, that is, actions that you should do just because they are right to do. Briefly explain why you believe each duty is important.

a.

b.

c.

d.

e.

Basing Morality on Virtues

A final ethical principle focuses on the role of moral virtues. A **virtue** is an ideal character trait that people should try to incorporate into their lives; it is a trait commonly found in ethically mature people. These traits are considered good in themselves, not good because of their consequences. Examples of ethical virtues include ideals such as honesty, loyalty, respect, responsibility, self-discipline, compassion, and courage. An action that is consistent with virtues like those is considered to be good, or moral. An action that conflicts with such virtues is considered bad, or immoral.

The Principle of Virtues

The **principle of virtues** states that ethics is based on being a good person, that is, on incorporating ideal character traits into your life. But how do you do that? How do you become honest with, responsible to, or generous toward others? Over 2,500 years ago, the Greek philosopher Aristotle wrote that the key is simply to make the virtues habits. In other words, if you don't think of yourself as an especially kind person, make up your mind to do one act of kindness today. Then do another kind act tomorrow, and so on. Eventually kindness will become a habit to you; at that point, kindness will have become ingrained into your character. You will be a kind person.

Thus, this principle would judge stealing money from the cash register at work to be wrong because doing so conflicts with the ethical virtues of honesty, integrity, and fairness. (See Illustration 2-6.) Whether this particular act of stealing would have good or bad consequences does not matter. And one's moral duties and the rights of others are not especially relevant. The principle of virtues would judge stealing to be inherently bad because it is inconsistent with the kind of person you should want to be.

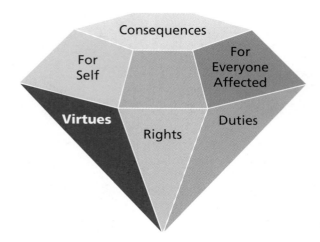

Principles for making ethical decisions

Illustration 2-6

Then how is a virtue defined? Precisely what does it mean to be courageous or generous? How do you know when you have achieved kindness or truthfulness? Aristotle addressed those questions with a unique concept called the **Golden Mean**, his way of defining virtues as perfect balances between opposite and undesirable extremes.

If you want to know exactly what it means to be courageous, you have to determine the undesirable extremes. What is the word for not having enough courage? Cowardice. That is one extreme. But can a person have too much courage? Aristotle said yes. There is an opposite extreme of courage to the point that the behavior doesn't make sense. It might be referred to as foolhardiness, that is, taking irrational, unnecessary risks to one's safety. Real courage, the virtue that you should try to incorporate into your life, is perfectly balanced between the two extremes. (See illustration 2-7.)

Cowardice   Courage   Foolhardiness

Illustration 2-7

> "Wisdom, compassion and courage— these are the three universally recognized moral qualities of men."
> —Confucius

Strengths and Weaknesses of the Principle of Virtues

A strength of using virtues as a basis for making decisions is that the virtues encourage people to achieve high levels of moral behavior. Some philosophers of ethics, including Plato and Aristotle, have maintained that the key to becoming a morally mature person is acting on virtues until they become habits. However, the principle also has its weaknesses. One problem is that some actions might promote one virtue while violating another. In addition, when such a conflict exists, people do not always agree on which virtues are most important. For example, if a friend asked you to tell a lie to cover up something that she had done, you would be forced to choose between the competing virtues of loyalty and honesty. When virtues alone are used to find answers to ethical questions, there may be no way to resolve the conflicts.

Ethics & Law

Free societies face a constant tug-of-war between the rights of individuals and the overall welfare of the larger group. Many state and federal laws were written specifically to protect individual rights. However, some laws are written to protect the interests of the larger group, even at the expense of individual rights. Eminent domain laws allow the government to take private property from individuals for the benefit of the community or society. The city government could take your house (paying you what it decides is a fair price) and use your land to build a road or a school, for example. Some courts have even ruled that individuals' land could be used to build a shopping center.

Checkpoint

1. Define the word *virtue*.

_____

_____

_____

2. Define the concept of the Golden Mean.

_____

_____

_____

3. Complete the Golden Mean continuum for the following virtues:

|———————————————— Generosity ————————————————|

|———————————————— Caring ————————————————|

|———————————————— Truthfulness ————————————————|

4. List one strength and one weaknesses of relying only on the principle of virtues when facing ethical questions.

_____

_____

_____

_____

_____

What do you think now?

If Joelle based her decision on moral virtues, what would she think about in making her decision? Which virtues do you think would be the most important and relevant? Why?

_____
_____
_____
_____
_____
_____
_____
_____
_____
_____
_____

Personal Reflection

1. List 12 essential virtues of a good, ethical life.
2. Review your list of virtues.

   a. Put an X beside those virtues that you believe are your strengths.

   b. Circle those virtues that you would like to exhibit more consistently.

"Inability to tell good from evil is the greatest worry of man's life."

—Cicero

Real-World Ethics

©Comstock Images

America's biggest shopping day of the year is the Friday following Thanksgiving Day. However, you might be surprised to learn that the biggest *online* shopping day of the year is the following Monday. Evidently, many people wait until they are back to work to go online and order gifts for the holidays. Remember, many of these people just had several days at home when they could have completed their online shopping. The theory is that work computers are generally faster than home computers, which explains why people wait until they are back at work to do their online shopping. Meanwhile, many employers have policies that forbid employees from using their work computers for personal matters such as shopping.

Is it ethically wrong for employees to use company computers for Internet shopping? Are employers justified in forbidding it? Explain.

Summary

Consequences are the effects or results of what a person does. The egoism principle maintains that an ethical action is the one that has the best consequences for a person. The utility principle argues that the right thing to do in any situation is the action that produces the most good or happiness for the most people.

The principle of rights maintains that an action is considered moral when it respects the rights of others; an action is considered immoral when it violates another's rights.

The principle of duties maintains that people should do what is ethically right purely because they have a moral obligation to do what is ethically right. They should do the right thing because it's the right thing to do.

The principle of virtues states that ethics is based on being a good person, that is, on incorporating ideal character traits into one's life.

Chapter 2 Assessments

Vocabulary Builder

Match the following terms to their definitions.

1. _____ An action is considered moral when it respects the rights of others; it is considered immoral when it violates another's rights.
2. _____ The method of defining virtues as perfect balances between opposite and undesirable extremes.
3. _____ An ethical obligation that one individual has to others.
4. _____ The idea that ethics is based on being a good person, on incorporating ideal character traits into one's life.
5. _____ An ideal character trait that people should try to incorporate in their lives; a trait commonly found in ethically mature people.
6. _____ The idea that it is wrong to use other people in ways that harm them for one's own benefit.
7. _____ The idea that the morally right action is the one that produces the best consequences for everyone involved, not just for one individual.
8. _____ The idea that people should act as they would want others to act in the same situation.
9. _____ The idea that people should do what is ethically right purely because they have a moral obligation to do what is ethically right.
10. _____ The effects or results of what people do.
11. _____ The idea that the right thing for a person to do in any situation is the action that best serves that person's long-term interests.
12. _____ A term used to describe how an individual is entitled to be treated by others.
13. _____ A way of viewing ethical right and wrong, often unique to an individual, a culture, or a subculture.

a. value system
b. consequences
c. egoism principle
d. utility principle
e. right
f. principle of rights
g. duty
h. principle of duties
i. universality
j. respect for persons
k. virtue
l. principle of virtues
m. Golden Mean

Reinforcement

1. List the five central ethical principles discussed in this chapter. Give one example of each.

_____

_____

_____

2. Match the following ethical principles to the correct statements.

_____ People should act in their own long-term best interests.
_____ People should act to produce the best consequences for the greatest number of people.
_____ People should do what is right because they have an obligation to do what is right.
_____ People should incorporate good character traits into their lives and keep striving to be good.
_____ People should respect and never violate the rights of others.

a. principle of duties
b. egoism principle
c. principle of rights
d. utility principle
e. principle of virtues

Thinking Critically

1. Toshi is a sophomore at a local community college. She also has a part-time job as an aide in the mayor's office. Yesterday a large, beautifully wrapped box was delivered to the office. Inside the box were dozens of expensive watches, gifts to the mayor's staff from the Tik-Tok Watch Corporation. Toshi knew that for the past few weeks, the city government had been debating a change in local zoning laws. Changing the laws would allow Tik-Tok to save millions of dollars when purchasing land for a new factory. Local officials, business leaders, and citizens were bitterly divided over the issue. No one was sure how the final vote by city council would turn out.

Toshi saw a card attached to the box. The card read, "Dear friends at City Hall: We at Tik-Tok are excited that we may soon be building a new factory in your community. We appreciate whatever help you can give us in getting the zoning laws changed. Please keep the watches as a token of our goodwill and friendship." As Toshi finished reading the card, she heard one of the other staffers call out, "Hey, Toshi. Do you want a gold watch, a silver watch, or both?"

Apply the ethical principles that you learned in this chapter. Then explain what Toshi should do about the situation in which she finds herself.

a. Egoism principle. What action would seem to be in Toshi's long-term best interests? Why?

_____

_____

_____

b. Utility principle. What could Toshi do that would produce the most overall good or happiness for the most people? Why?

_____

_____

_____

c. Principle of rights. Whose rights are at stake in this situation? How might Toshi's actions violate another's rights? Explain.

_____

_____

_____

d. Principle of duties. What moral duties does Toshi have that are relevant to this situation? What action seems most consistent with those duties? Why?

_____

_____

_____

e. Principle of virtues. What moral virtues are relevant to Toshi's situation? What action by Toshi would seem to promote the most virtues?

_____

_____

_____

Now put it all together. What do you think Toshi should do about the watches from Tik-Tok? Explain your answer, using points from the ethical principles.

_____

_____

_____

_____

2. Nick has an old car that barely runs. He wants to get rid of it. His neighbor, Frisco, knows very little about cars. Nick is thinking about trying to con Frisco into buying the car. Nick knows he will have to lie about the condition of the car; otherwise, Frisco won't consider buying it.

What is Nick likely to do if he tries to follow the concept of universality? Explain your answer.

_____

_____

_____

_____

What is Nick likely to do if he tries to follow the concept of respect for persons? Explain your answer.

_____

_____

_____

_____

Digging Deeper

1. Watch the national and local news on television for several days. Keep track of stories that focus on important ethical issues. Note any references made to the principles of egoism, utility, duties, rights, or virtues. Which principles are mentioned most often? Why do you think that is so? Write a one-page summary of your findings. Be prepared to discuss them with your classmates.

2. As a class, pick one ethical issue that is controversial among students at your school. Survey students, asking what their opinions are about the issue and why they think the way they do. Keep track of how many references you hear to the principles of egoism, utility, duties, rights, and virtues. Which principles are most common? least common? Why do you think that is so? Write an article about your survey. If your school publishes a newspaper, check with your teacher to see if your article can be included in an upcoming issue.

3. Give an example of a recent movie that deals with ethical issues or in which the characters have to make important ethical decisions. Which principles do the characters use? Does the movie portray some principles as being better than others? If so, do you think those principles really are better? Write a one-page paper summarizing your thoughts.

4. Different countries, cultures, and subcultures often have different ways of looking at morality.

   a. Interview people at your school who have lived in other countries. Ask them for examples of how people in other countries view certain ethical issues differently than people in the United States. Do different cultures seem to favor different ethical principles? Summarize your findings in a one-page paper and bring it to class for discussion.

   b. Interview people at your school from different subcultures (racial, religious, ethnic, and so on). Ask them for examples of how people in different subcultures within the United States look at moral issues in different ways. Do different subcultures seem to favor different ethical principles? Write a one-page paper about what you learn.

Personal Reflection

1. Think of a time recently when you faced a difficult ethical question or problem. How did you decide what to do?

   a. The ethical decision I made had to do with the question or problem of

   b. When I look back on how I made my decision, the principles that I relied on most were

   c. If I had it to do over again today, I would change the following about how I made my decision:

2. Look back at the Personal Reflection on page 39. Choose one of the virtues you circled that you most want to incorporate into your life. For one week, concentrate on doing at least one act each day that promotes that virtue. Record your daily deeds on the lines below. At the end of the week, summarize your feelings about the experience and your accomplishments.

   Day 1:

   Day 2:

   Day 3:

   Day 4:

   Day 5:

   Day 6:

   Day 7:

   End of week summary:

3. The most important ideas that I learned from this chapter were

4. I would like to investigate further and learn more about

5. I think I could use some of the principles in this chapter to help me make a decision about

Personal Ethical Development

Chapter Goals

After completing this chapter, you should be able to:

- Explain the components of consistent ethical behavior.
- Describe stages in the Justice Model of personal ethical development.
- Describe steps in the Caring Model of personal ethical development.
- Explain the roles of the opposing inner forces that help determine a person's ethical development.

Key Terms & Concepts

moral sensitivity	justice	caring
ethical judgment	moral development	inner conflict
ethical motivation	social contract	fear of change
ethical character	universal ethical principles	

What do you think?

Will has a summer job working for the local electric company. He has been assigned to the warehouse, where the company stores all of the parts and equipment used to maintain the power lines and to keep electricity running. His job is to help load and unload the trucks; to keep the shelves stocked; and to run occasional errands for the warehouse supervisor, Mr. Walker.

The atmosphere is tense around the power company this summer. The union and management have been fighting over a new contract; and from what Will can tell, management seems to be winning. The employees are angry and bitter.

While completing a parts inventory one day, Will noticed that many of the shelves were bare. A lot of equipment seemed to be missing. When he reported his findings to Mr. Walker, the supervisor told Will not to worry.

"I've seen this kind of thing before. It's just the line workers' way of getting even with management. If the workers don't get paid what they think they deserve, they make up for it by stealing equipment from the warehouse and off the trucks. It's not really right, but frankly, I'm on their side. The company is not being fair. So we'll help hide the missing materials and keep the workers out of trouble. Just change your inventory reports to show that we're missing only a little each month. With a little luck, the contract negotiations will be over by the time the company catches on to what's happening."

Will realizes that Mr. Walker is telling him to lie on important company documents. Will doesn't want to make his supervisor angry, but Will has to sign the documents. He can get into serious trouble if he is caught turning in fraudulent inventory reports. After all, doing so is not just a violation of company policy; it's against the law!

Will found this job through a good friend of his mom's—Ms. Davidoff, a company vice president—a fact he has kept from Mr. Walker. Reporting what he knows to her could make things very difficult for him at the company, but he also might receive some kind of reward. On the other hand, Will has made a lot of new friends at the company and he doesn't want them to hate him.

It seems as though all of Will's options have strong pros and cons. What should he do? Why?

You have probably noticed that babies and very young children do not seem to have any concept of moral right and wrong. They don't seem to feel shame or guilt. They don't seem particularly proud when they do the right thing. They don't even know that there is a right thing.

Yet most teenagers and adults do have an inner understanding of ethics. Granted, some people's conceptions of right and wrong seem strange, but at least they know right from wrong. Have you ever wondered how people acquire an understanding of morality or how it develops? Did you know that there is more than one theory about how this understanding of morality works? In this chapter, you'll explore possible answers to those questions and more. You'll also discover strategies for measuring how morally mature you are now and learn ways to grow in this area in the future.

You Decide

Here are five situations, each requiring a decision. For each scenario, answer yes or no and then explain why you made that choice. Be honest with yourself. You may share your responses with others if you choose, but you may also decide to keep them to yourself.

1. Your good friend Ellen asks you to casually mention to her parents that she was at your house Saturday night. You don't know where she was. Would you go along with her request and be her alibi?

Yes or no? _____

Why or why not? _____

_____

_____

2. You are not doing very well in algebra, and a big test is scheduled for tomorrow. A reliable classmate shows you a copy of the test that he says he found near the school copy machine. Would you use the test to help you get a better grade?

Yes or no? _____

Why or why not? _____

_____

_____

3. After six games, your school's football team is undefeated and has a chance to get into the state playoffs. You learn that, without a doubt, two of the star players are using illegal steroids. Would you inform an appropriate authority?

Yes or no? _____

Why or why not? _____

_____

_____

4. You work at a clothing store at the mall. One day you see a coworker, whom you were starting to think of as a friend, take some clothes and put them in the trunk of her car. She tells you not to worry about it. "It's no big deal. Everyone here takes a few things home from time to time. This chain makes millions and pays us next to nothing. We deserve more, and this is how we get it." Would you report the theft?

Yes or no? _____

Why or why not? _____

_____

_____

5. Same situation as #4. Would you start taking merchandise home with you, too?

Yes or no? _____

Why or why not? _____

_____

_____

Personal Reflection

Take a minute to look back over your answers. How do you feel about them?

1. As promised, you don't have to share your answers with anyone, but how would you feel if you did? Which answers would you be at least a little embarrassed for your friends to see? your teacher? your parents?

2. Imagine that after writing all your answers you found out that this exercise was part of a job interview. Would you want to change any answers before you gave it to the interviewer? What does that tell you?

3. Now imagine that you are an employer conducting job interviews. Your responses belong to an applicant whom you haven't seen yet. Looking at your answers, would you hire that person to work for you? How does your answer to that question make you feel?

Components of Consistent Ethical Behavior

James Rest (1941–1999) was a leader in research on personal ethical development. He noted that there are four basic components to a person maintaining consistent ethical behavior. You'll see that those four components build on one another.

Moral Sensitivity

Imagine that you're playing catch with a friend in a street near your home. Your friend is hard of hearing. At some point, you notice a car coming up the street behind your friend. The car is moving fast, and it is swerving. You realize that your friend is in immediate danger, but he doesn't yet sense that something is wrong.

Ethical issues can sometimes be like that. **Moral sensitivity** is the ability to recognize the presence of ethical issues, questions, and temptations. Moral sensitivity is not something to be taken for granted; not everyone has it. In the business world, it's not unusual to see someone's career end for an ethical misdeed that he or she didn't recognize as a matter of right or wrong. The person never saw the car that hit him or her.

For example, just a couple of decades ago, sexual harassment was largely tolerated in the workplace. Far too many women (and men) were subjected to inappropriate and repeated sexual advances, offers of promotions in exchange for such favors, and threats of being fired if they reported the outrageous actions. Such behavior was never acceptable or right, and there were no excuses that justified it. But that's how the work environment was and had been for so long that many people felt powerless to do anything about the situation, except, perhaps, to change jobs and hope that the next boss would be better.

Fortunately, sexual harassment laws and lawsuits have resulted in more professional office environments. Everyone has the right to work in an atmosphere free of intimidation and harassment. Companies are now held legally liable for the actions of their employees. Harassers may be fired, may be sued, or may find their careers in tatters before they come to realize that the car was swerving their way.

The first component necessary to be an ethical person is to have the sensitivity to recognize an ethical problem when you see one. (See Illustration 3-1.) But that's not enough, is it? A person can realize that he or she is dealing with an ethical issue and still not know what to do about it.

Ethical Sensitivity

Illustration 3-1

Ethical Judgment

Ethical judgment is the ability to decide on the best or right course of action—to be able to make a responsible ethical judgment. So you think to yourself, Is it ethically right or wrong to sexually harass people? Hmmm, let me think. Wait, give me a minute; I'll get it!

If you're honest with yourself, you don't usually have to think too hard to know what's right and wrong. You generally know right away. People shouldn't cheat, lie, or sexually harass people. People should be courageous enough to do the right thing in difficult situations and try to help others in need. But there are times when decisions are more complicated than that. What if cheating on a final exam is the only way to graduate and be accepted into college? What about lying to protect someone from danger? Does a person's duty to help others in need mean that he or she should give a ride to a stranger who is standing on the side of a dark highway?

It's important to be able to determine the most ethical course of action in a situation. (See Illustration 3-2.) But that's not enough all by itself. Many times in life people know the right thing to do; they just don't want to do it.

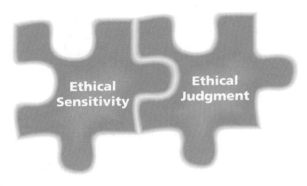

Illustration 3-2

"To see what is right and not do it is cowardice."

—Confucius

Ethical Motivation

To be a consistently ethical person, you have to have **ethical motivation**, that is, the personal disposition to do the right thing. You have to have a strong inner desire to be a good person and to live a good life. You have to want that more than you want the immediate and short-term rewards that unethical actions can sometimes bring.

Think back to the question about the coworker who encouraged you to steal clothes from the store where you worked. You recognized immediately that stealing was an ethical problem, and your conscience reminded you that stealing was wrong. Still, you may find yourself being tempted to do the wrong thing at times. The only thing that keeps you out of trouble is that inner desire to do the right thing.

However, just wanting to do the right thing may not be enough either. Sometimes you recognize an ethical temptation, know the right thing to do, and even want to do what's right—but still end up doing what you knew was wrong. (See Illustration 3-3.) That means there has to be one more component.

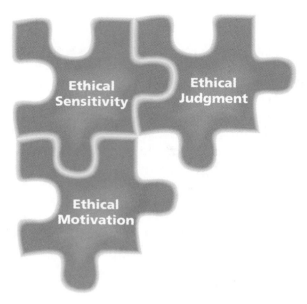

Illustration 3-3

Ethical Character

What if ALL of the other employees at that store were stealing? It turns out they are actually an organized ring of employee thieves! And not only are they encouraging you to join them, they are demanding it. They threaten to harm you and your family if you tell anyone what you know. And you believe they would.

Ethical character means having the self-discipline and courage to follow through in difficult situations and to do what you know you should, even under extreme pressure. Life isn't fair, and sometimes people end up in difficult situations. Do you have the courage to stand alone and report the ring of thieves? Do you have the self-discipline to study twice as hard for the exam so you don't have to cheat? Do you have the character to fail the class and delay your graduation in order to keep your integrity? (See Illustration 3-4.)

Learn More

Use an Internet search engine to find one or two web sites about James Rest. Bring to class one new fact that you find.

Illustration 3-4

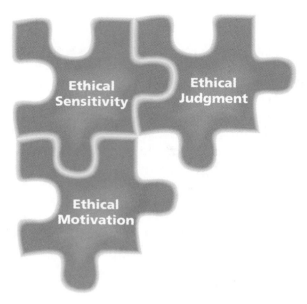

Those are very difficult, life-altering decisions, and not everyone is ethically mature enough to make the right decision and follow through with his or her convictions. What makes one person more ethically mature than another? How can individuals become more ethically mature than they are now? Those are the next questions to which you will learn answers.

Checkpoint

1. In your own words, summarize the meanings of Rest's four components of consistent ethical behavior.

a. moral sensitivity: _____

_____

b. ethical judgment: _____

_____

c. ethical motivation: _____

_____

d. ethical character: _____

_____

2. In your opinion, which is the easiest to develop? Why?

_____

_____

3. In your opinion, which is the hardest to develop? Why?

_____

_____

What do you think now?

Think back to Will's scenario at the beginning of the chapter. Explain how each of Rest's components could affect how Will perceives the situation and what Will might do about it.

1. How would having developed moral sensitivity affect Will's perceptions of the situation?

_____

_____

2. How would having the ability to make good ethical judgments affect Will's decision about what to do?

_____

_____

3. How would having ethical motivation make a difference in Will's actions?

_____

_____

4. How would having developed ethical character affect how Will follows through in the situation?

_____

_____

Personal Reflection

1. Which components do you see as strengths of yours?

2. Which components do you see as weaknesses of yours?

3. What are three things you could do to improve those areas of weakness?
   a.

   b.

   c.

Clearly, not everyone is at the same place in his or her personal ethical development. But it might surprise you to learn that researchers have been studying for decades how humans develop the understanding of moral right and wrong. Several competing theories have been proposed to explain how the process works. This section will explore two of those theories—the Justice Model and the Caring Model.

The Justice Model of Moral Development

Justice refers to impartial fairness, or equity. The first model of moral development uses justice as the main criteria in measuring a person's moral maturity. Thus, ethical decisions that are based on self-interest and unfairness would be considered immature.

Lawrence Kohlberg (1927–1987) was an American psychologist who dedicated his career to understanding human **moral development**, the process of growing more ethically mature. He wondered whether people's ideas about moral right and wrong were based only on what they were taught or whether some of those ideas were _innate,_ meaning somehow built into people. Kohlberg wondered whether the ethical maturing process was the same for all humans or whether it varied by individuals, groups, or countries. To find out, Kohlberg studied and interviewed thousands of children from many different nations, cultures, and religious groups.

Typically, Kohlberg would present each child with a case study of a character facing an ethical dilemma. He would ask the child what the character should do in the situation and why. His assumption was that the answer to the *why* question held the key to understanding the child's moral reasoning and, thus, to understanding the child's level of moral development.

Kohlberg's research led him to identify six stages of human moral development. One of his most interesting conclusions was that those six stages seem to exist everywhere. Children from different cultures and religious groups progress through the same sequence of stages of moral reasoning. That finding implies that a person's sense of morality may not be limited just to what he or she is taught by others. Like the sequence in physical development of sitting up, crawling, walking, and running, the stages of moral development may somehow be programmed into a person.

Stage 1—Punishment and Obedience

In Kohlberg's first stage, right and wrong are perceived in terms of the physical consequences of particular actions. (See Illustration 3-5.) Actions that lead to pleasant consequences are considered good, and actions that lead to unpleasant consequences are considered bad. Most children learn early in life that disobedience to authority figures (parents) leads to punishment (unpleasant), while obedience leads to praise (pleasant). Soon morality comes to be thought of in terms of obedience to authority and avoidance of punishment.

Lawrence Kohlberg

Illustration 3-5

Many children understand that hurting others is wrong, but they often give different reasons when asked why. Typically, children in Stage 1 think of the action as wrong because their parents have told them not to do it and because those who hurt others get punished. Notice that self-centeredness is at the heart of this way of reasoning. Children in this stage do not understand that other people have feelings and needs like their own; therefore, the children are not capable of sympathy or compassion. The only motivating force is avoiding punishment.

> "Character builds slowly, but it can be torn down with incredible swiftness."
> —Faith Baldwin

Stage 2—Instrument and Relativity

A child in Kohlberg's second stage has a more realistic view of others. (See Illustration 3-6.) Now other people are seen as having feelings and needs like the child, but the child is still motivated by self-centeredness. These children think of a right action as one that meets their needs and desires. In other words, morally right actions are the tools (instruments) used to meet personal needs. Therefore, Stage 2 children can be manipulative, using the feelings and needs of others to get what they want. Morality is seen as relative, meaning that it changes according to different situations.

Lawrence Kohlberg

Illustration 3-6

For example, consider a young girl whose room is a mess. Her parents are expecting company soon and are anxious about what the visitors will think if the house doesn't look neat and clean. In Stage 2, avoiding punishment is less likely to be the reason the girl would clean her room. She is more likely to notice the stress and tension that her parents are feeling and try to bargain with them, perhaps cleaning her room in exchange for money or some other reward.

Stage 3—Interpersonal Concordance

In Kohlberg's third stage, individuals feel a strong need to be liked, accepted, and thought well of by others. (See Illustration 3-7.) The word *concordance* means "agreement or harmony." So morally right actions are thought of as those that gain social approval. Wrong actions are those that bring social condemnation, embarrassment, or rejection. Thus, people in Stage 3 are strongly influenced by peer pressure. The peer group may even replace parents as the primary moral authority. After all, the peer group decides what actions lead to social approval and what actions lead to disapproval.

Consider the not unusual case of a 14-year-old boy who starts smoking cigarettes, drinking alcohol, or experimenting with drugs because his peer group encourages him to do so. Stage 3 reasoning leads him to think that his actions are

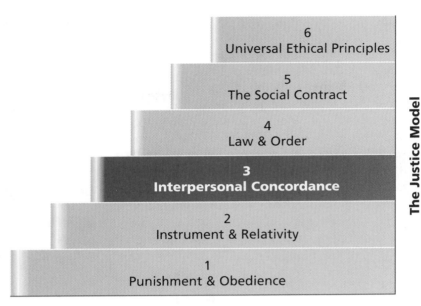

Lawrence Kohlberg

Illustration 3-7

right because of the way the group treats him when he does what it expects. Unlike Stage 1 and Stage 2 children, he is willing to sacrifice his own physical self-interest to please the group and gain its approval.

Stage 4—Law and Order

People in Kohlberg's fourth stage have developed a mature view of the world. (See Illustration 3-8.) People see the world as being much bigger than their individual peer groups. Stage 4 people understand that they are part of a larger

Lawrence Kohlberg

Illustration 3-8

community, and they feel a moral duty to maintain the order and stability of that community. An action that promotes the harmony and smooth functioning of society is seen as right. An action that interferes with the social order is seen as wrong. As a result, individuals in Stage 4 have a strong sense of citizenship, duty, responsibility, and obedience to the laws of the land.

While reasoning at this stage is at a higher level than at the previous stages, it does have a flaw. People in Stage 4 sometimes think of the government as the ultimate moral authority. They define the role of a citizen as obeying that authority. (See Illustration 3-9.) Therefore, these individuals may lack the ability to understand the differences between just and unjust laws. They may conclude that if an action is legally right, it must be morally right as well. As in Stage 3, the emphasis is on conformity. Now, however, the conformity is to the laws made by government, not just the will of the peer group. Stage 4 reasoning makes it difficult for a person to understand the need to challenge abuses of authority or to protest unfair laws.

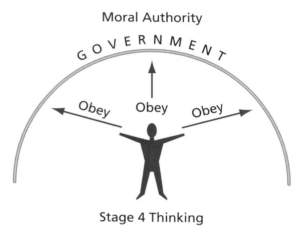

Moral Authority

GOVERNMENT

Obey   Obey   Obey

Stage 4 Thinking

Illustration 3-9

Ethics & Law

- Provide two examples of historic American laws that most people now believe were unjust or morally wrong.

- Provide one example of a current American law that some people argue is unjust.

- What is the ethical response for a person confronted with laws that he or she is convinced are unjust?

"Never do anything against conscience, even if the state demands it."
—Albert Einstein

Stage 5—The Social Contract

Individuals in Kohlberg's fifth stage view the government as a legal authority, not a moral one. (See Illustration 3-10.) They believe that there is a higher moral authority, the **social contract**, which represents the deepest values and beliefs of a society. The government's role is seen as serving the will of the people. (See Illustration 3-11.) When the government fails to live up to that responsibility, the role of citizenship is to question, challenge, and even change the government if necessary.

Lawrence Kohlberg

Illustration 3-10

Because they reason about ethics in this way, individuals in Stage 5 often take on the role of protesters. They view morality in terms of important social values. In America, those values might include beliefs in the equality of all people, the dignity and worth of the individual, human rights, and fairness. But note that other societies and cultures would have different values and beliefs and, therefore, would have different social contracts.

Illustration 3-11

Stage 6—Universal Ethical Principles

People at Kohlberg's highest level of moral development view right and wrong in terms of **universal ethical principles**. (See Illustration 3-12.) These are ethical principles that are self-chosen (no one forces a person to choose them) and universal (other people thinking rationally would have to agree that the principles are worthy). These principles could include some of those discussed in Chapter 2, especially principles dealing with justice or fairness to others. These principles include respecting the worth and value of human life, acting as you would want others to act, and believing in the importance of individual rights. People in Stage 5 might follow these principles also, but only if the principles are part of society's social contract. People in Stage 6 would rely on these principles no matter what kind of society they found themselves in.

Lawrence Kohlberg

Illustration 3-12

Learn More

Use an Internet search engine to find one or two web sites about Lawrence Kohlberg and his theory of moral development. Bring to class one new fact that you find.

Kohlberg believed that very few people ever reach this final stage of moral development. People in this stage feel compelled by personal ethical principles to rise above the values and beliefs of their societies. (See Illustration 3-13.)

Stage 6 Thinking

Illustration 3-13

They are willing to sacrifice their own needs, interests, and sometimes their lives to try to pull their societies up to a higher moral plane. Kohlberg frequently mentioned Mahatma Gandhi of India and Martin Luther King, Jr., of the United States as examples of people demonstrating Stage 6 reasoning.

Checkpoint

1. What does the word *justice* mean to you?

_____

_____

2. In your own words, write the main idea of each of Kohlberg's stages of ethical development.

a. To a person in Stage 1, ethical right and wrong are based on

_____

_____

b. Stage 2 reasoning would lead a person to think that actions are right or wrong based on

_____

_____

c. To a person in Stage 3, what makes actions right and wrong is based on

_____

_____

d. People in Stage 4 would tend to think that ethical right and wrong are based on

_____

_____

e. A person in Stage 5 would base right and wrong on

_____

_____

f. Stage 6 reasoning about ethical right and wrong is based on

_____

_____

3. Kohlberg assumed that a person's ethical maturity is based less on their ethical behavior than on how they think or reason about right and wrong. Do you agree? Why or why not?

_____

_____

Think back to the scenario involving Will at the beginning of the chapter. Use the following table to apply Kohlberg's stages to Will's decision. How would Will be reasoning about right and wrong at each stage? What might he decide to do at each stage?

	The Justice Model	
Stage	**What Would Will Be Thinking?**	**What Might Will Do? Why?**
1		
2		
3		
4		
5		
6		

Personal Reflection

Go back to the beginning of the chapter and look at your answers to "You Decide." Don't be concerned with the yes or no responses. Instead, focus on your answers to the *why* questions. Try to match each reason you gave to one of Kohlberg's stages. Here's an example.

You are not doing very well in algebra, and a big test is scheduled for tomorrow. A reliable classmate shows you a copy of the test that he says he found near the school copy machine. Would you use this test to help you get a better grade?

Yes/No?

Why/Why Not?

Be forewarned that it takes some maturity to be that honest with yourself. After matching all five responses to Kohlberg's stages, consider these questions.

1. Which stages appear most often? least often? What does that tell you about yourself and your current level of ethical maturity?

2. Write one life change that you could make that might help you mature in your understanding of justice or fairness and how you express them in your life.

While Kohlberg's Justice Model has been praised as an important first step in understanding the process of moral development, it has also been criticized. The strongest criticism has come from feminist scholars who were offended that Kohlberg's own evaluations of people tended to score women lower in ethical development than men. The scholars have claimed that Kohlberg's model may describe male moral development but that it does not apply as well to women.

One of this group's most influential spokespersons has been Carol Gilligan (1936–present). She has created a competing model based on what she believes to be at the heart of how women view ethics, the concept of caring.

The Caring Model of Moral Development

Caring means "looking out for the interests of someone or something." Since Gilligan uses a different standard for measuring moral maturity, it is not surprising that the stages or steps in her theory also differ. Thus, her approach views moral development as a three-step process, with each step defined by how people care about and relate to others.

Step One: Self—Centeredness

The first step in the Caring Model is characterized by self-interest. (See Illustration 3-14.) People at this level care about meeting only their own needs

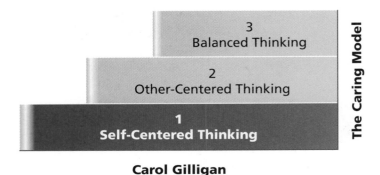

Carol Gilligan

Illustration 3-14

"The essence of ethics is some level of caring."

—Michael Josephson

and interests, at the expense of others if necessary. This attitude is usually expressed in acts of selfishness, a lack of concern for others, and in actions that exploit or manipulate others for personal gain.

Step Two: Others—Centeredness

People at Gilligan's second step feel obligated to ignore their own needs and interests to meet the needs of others. (See Illustration 3-15.) In other words, the pendulum has now swung from being self-centered at the expense of others to being others-centered at the expense of oneself. Sometimes this attitude is referred to as the *martyr syndrome.* This is the mistaken belief that seeing yourself as a "good person" requires having to sacrifice yourself or your needs for others.

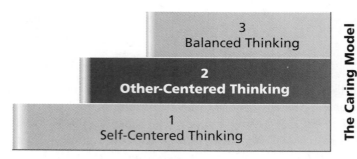

Carol Gilligan

Illustration 3-15

Learn More

Use an Internet search engine to find one or two web sites about Carol Gilligan and her theory. Bring to class one new fact that you find.

People at this level often feel guilty when they do something nice for themselves. They don't seem to think that they deserve it. However, Gilligan's point is that people must understand that moral maturity is based on more than self-denial before they can move on to the third and final step.

Step Three: Balancing Needs

The third step in the Caring Model is characterized by a sense of balance and flexibility. (See Illustration 3-16.) According to Gilligan, morally mature people understand that living a complete life means finding ways to meet their own needs and interests as well as the needs and interests of others who are close to them. Such people understand that they do not have to feel guilty for trying to meet their own needs. They understand ethics not in terms of caring for me *or* them, but for me *and* them.

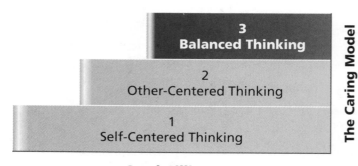

Carol Gilligan

Illustration 3-16

Checkpoint

1. What does the word *caring* mean to you?

_____

_____

2. In your own words, write the main idea of the three steps in the Caring Model.

a. To a person in Step One, ethical right and wrong are based on

_____

_____

b. On what would a person in Step Two tend to think that ethical right and wrong are based?

_____

_____

c. Step Three reasoning would indicate that ethical right and wrong are based on

_____

_____

3. Have your own experiences in life generally supported Carol Gilligan's assumption that women tend to think and reason about ethics differently than men? If so, give two or three examples.

_____

_____

What do you think now?

Take another look at Will's scenario at the beginning of the chapter. Apply Gilligan's stages to his decision. How would Will be reasoning about right and wrong at each stage? What might he decide to do at each step?

The Caring Model		
Step	**What Would Will Be Thinking?**	**What Might Will Do?**
One		
Two		
Three		

Personal Reflection

Think back again to your *why* responses to the You Decide scenarios. This time, though, determine which step in Gilligan's theory best fits each of your answers. Here's an example.

After six games, your school's football team is undefeated and has a chance to get into the state playoffs. You learn that, without a doubt, two of the star players are using illegal steroids. Would you inform an appropriate authority?

Yes/No?

Why/Why Not?

After matching all five *why* responses with steps in Gilligan's theory, consider these questions.

1. Which step appears most often? least often? What does that tell you about yourself and your current level of ethical maturity?

2. What similarities and differences do you see between how you rated in the Justice and Caring Models? Did you score better on one than the other? If so, why do you suppose that is true?

3. Write one change that you could make to help you mature in your understanding of caring and the way you express it in your life.

"We cannot learn without pain."
—Aristotle

Opposing Forces

Two opposing forces are at work in the process of personal ethical development. (See Illustration 3-17.) In all developmental theories, it is normal and expected that people will keep moving from one stage or step to the next. So some inner force must be involved, constantly pushing people toward higher stages of ethical reasoning. This first force is **inner conflict**.

When something about a person's present stage isn't working well for him or her, the person is left with a sense of frustration or anxiety. That inner conflict motivates the person to look for different ways of thinking. That is why most people can look back over their lives and see that the difficult times were often the times

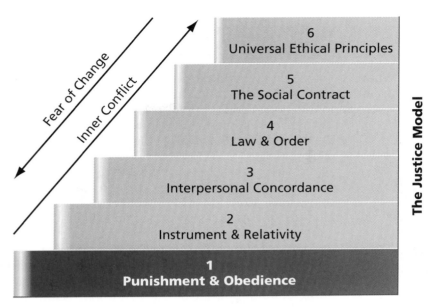

The Justice Model

Fear of Change

Inner Conflict

6
Universal Ethical Principles

5
The Social Contract

4
Law & Order

3
Interpersonal Concordance

2
Instrument & Relativity

1
Punishment & Obedience

Lawrence Kohlberg

Illustration 3-17

they grew the most. It also explains why people don't grow as much when their lives are comfortable and easy.

However, if inner conflict was the only force at work, everyone would get to the highest levels of ethical reasoning. After all, life provides many difficult times for everyone. So there has to be another competing force that prevents people from moving up. That second force is **fear of change**.

Many humans fear change more than almost anything else in life. And that fear has a paralyzing power. Haven't you seen or heard of a situation in which someone was in an unbearably bad life situation, but he or she stayed because the fear of change was even stronger than the agony with which the individual chose to live?

So when things are going well and people's lives are comfortable, inner conflict remains low and fear of change outweighs it. Therefore, people stay where they are. But when difficult times come and a person's current way of thinking is inadequate, his or her inner conflict rises. If that inner conflict gets stronger than the person's fear of change, he or she starts to grow and mature.

> "If there is no struggle, there is no progress."
> —Frederick Douglass

Personal Reflection

1. Think of time in your life when you went through a difficult experience. Explain how you grew as a person as a result of the ordeal.

2. Think of areas of your life with which you are not satisfied but in which you haven't been able to make the changes necessary to improve the situation. Describe one situation and what you can do to change it.

Real-World Ethics

©Getty Images/PhotoDisc

What would you do if you found a wallet that contained $100 in cash, a few credit cards, and a driver's license? Some people would keep the money and rationalize their decision by telling themselves that many other individuals would make the same choice. But, really, what would most people do?

Investigations to learn the answer to that question have been enlightening. Reporters on television news shows have intentionally left wallets on streets and used hidden cameras to see what people will do. On average, about 7 out of 10 people returned the wallets (with the contents) or turned the wallets in to authorities. In one case, a news show conducted the test on police officers in New York and Los Angeles. Every officer who found a "lost" billfold returned it to the "owner"—cash and all!

Summary

Being a consistently ethical person requires moral sensitivity, ethical judgment, ethical motivation, and ethical character.

Lawrence Kohlberg's theory of moral development measures a person's understanding of the concept of justice. The six stages of the Justice Model are:

1. Obey authority and avoid punishment.
2. Act in ways that meet your own needs and get you what you want.
3. Act in ways that get you social approval.
4. Conform to established rules, laws, and policies.
5. Follow the ethical principles and values of your society or culture.
6. Follow your own personal, but universal, ethical principles.

Carol Gilligan was convinced that the Justice Theory applied better to men than to women. Gilligan's theory of ethical development measures a person's understanding of the concept of caring. The three steps in the Caring Model are:

1. Caring for self only, at the expense of others if necessary
2. Caring for others only, at the expense of self if necessary
3. Balancing care for self and others

The two inner forces that have a lot to do with how far and how fast a person matures in his or her ethical development are inner conflict and fear of change.

Vocabulary Builder

Match the following terms to their definitions.

1. _____ The basis for Kohlberg's theory, meaning impartial fairness, or equity.
2. _____ The basis for Gilligan's theory, meaning a concern for the welfare of someone or something.
3. _____ The ability to recognize and identify ethical issues and problems.
4. _____ The ability to determine the morally right or best course of action.
5. _____ The inner desire to do the right thing, to be a good person.
6. _____ Possessing the personal courage and self-discipline to follow through and do what is right in situations of great temptation or pressure.
7. _____ The inner force that motivates people to move up toward higher levels of ethical thinking.
8. _____ The inner force that holds people back from personal growth, which keeps them where they are.

a. ethical judgment
b. moral sensitivity
c. caring
d. justice
e. ethical motivation
f. fear of change
g. inner conflict
h. ethical character

Reinforcement

1. What are the key components of consistent ethical character?

_____
_____
_____
_____

2. According to the Justice Model, what stages do people go through in their understanding of ethical right and wrong?

_____
_____
_____
_____

3. According to the Caring Model, what steps do people go through in their understanding of ethical right and wrong?

_____
_____
_____
_____

4. What inner forces help to determine how people will continue to mature in their ethical reasoning?

_____

_____

_____

_____

5. Read the following scenario. For each of Lee's statements, identify the correct stage of the Justice Model and provide an explanation. Do the same for the Caring Model.

Last Saturday Lee was arrested for trespassing during a protest rally at Nukes-R-Us, a plant that manufactures parts for atomic weapons and sells them to terrorists. During Lee's questioning, the police tried to determine which stage of moral development Lee was operating from, but he kept changing his story. Identify the correct stage of the Justice Model for each of Lee's statements.

The Justice Model

a. "This business is violating every principle that our country stands for! This is not what America is about. The government is wrong to allow companies like this to exist. We are going to stand up for what America believes in and protest until the government passes laws to make this kind of business illegal!"
Stage _____ because

_____

_____

_____

_____

b. "I'm really sorry about what happened, but it's not my fault. The leader of this group is vicious and dangerous. I had to go along with him, or I would have gotten into trouble. He might have hurt me."
Stage _____ because

_____

_____

_____

_____

c. "Look, all of my friends belong to this protest group. I couldn't let them down. What kind of person would they think I am if I didn't climb the fence with them? I don't want my friends thinking I'm a coward!"
Stage _____ because

_____

_____

_____

_____

d. "To be honest, I'm not really one of the protesters. Some guy paid a bunch of us $50 each if we would make the crowd look bigger for the television cameras. I'm just out for myself here. I'll even testify against them if you drop the charges against me and pay me a little something for my trouble."
Stage _____ because

_____

_____

_____

_____

e. "I cannot stand by silently while a company violates important principles that I believe in deeply. Human life is at stake. Arrest me if you have to, but I'm standing by my principles."
Stage _____ because

_____

_____

_____

_____

f. "I'm really an undercover police officer, not a protester. I was keeping an eye on the protesters. Personally, I believe that every law is a good law and that anyone who breaks a law on purpose has done something ethically wrong. Arrest them all!"
Stage _____ because

_____

_____

_____

_____

The Caring Model

a. "I don't care what happens to me. I was just here trying to keep my sister from getting into too much trouble. You can arrest me or whatever, but let her go. She's the one that matters."

Step _____ because

_____

_____

_____

_____

b. "The truth is that I don't really care what happens to all of these other people. I thought this experience would be good for me, and I accidentally got caught up in the craziness. I don't deserve to be arrested or punished. I don't care what you do with the rest of them, but I demand to be released!"

Step _____ because

_____

_____

_____

_____

c. "Look, I didn't come here to cause anyone grief. I care about the fact that my family and I live so close to a dangerous plant. I care about the people who might be harmed by the products it makes. I also care about the employees of this company. I don't want them to lose their jobs. Couldn't they just start making a different kind of product? Can't we find some kind of solution here that lets everyone benefit?"

Step _____ because

_____

_____

_____

_____

Thinking Critically

Juanita is a senior, only three weeks away from graduation ceremonies at her high school. She applied to a state university in a nearby city and was told that she will be accepted upon graduation from high school. Unfortunately, between her part-time job, her practice sessions and games with the basketball team, and her involvement in several clubs, Juanita has fallen behind in her schoolwork. She is now beginning to realize that she may not pass enough classes to graduate in the spring. Attending summer school is an option; but if she does that, her family won't be able to travel to Puerto Rico for its annual summer trip. Juanita doesn't want her family to miss the trip because of her.

Juanita has figured out that she will have enough credits to graduate only if she passes her senior composition class. To pass, she has to make an A on the class research paper that is due in two days. The problem is that she has not yet picked a topic or started her research. She has been too busy catching up in her other classes. Now she's beginning to panic.

Alan is a neighbor and friend who graduated from Juanita's school last year. He tells Juanita that he had the same teacher last year. Alan kept his research paper, on which he received an A. He offers to sell it to Juanita for $20. It turns out that Alan bought the paper for $15 from a cousin who wrote it for a college class.

How would Juanita reason through her decision according to each model of moral developments? What do you think she will do at each stage or step? Use the following tables to record your answers.

The Justice Model		
Stage	**What Is Juanita Thinking?**	**What Might Juanita Do? Why?**
1		
2		
3		
4		
5		
6		

The Caring Model		
Step	What Is Juanita Thinking?	What Might Juanita Do? Why?
One		
Two		
Three		

Digging Deeper

1. Look for newspaper, magazine, or Internet articles in which people talk about their ethical or unethical actions. Look for clues as to the possible levels of moral development of the people mentioned in the articles. Bring your favorite article to class for discussion.

2. Rent from a local video store or borrow from your local library the 1982 movie *Gandhi*. Look for characters in the film who represent each stage in the Justice Model and each step in the Caring Model. Write a one-page summary/reaction paper about the film.

3. List three movies or television shows that you saw recently that contained ethical themes. At what stages or steps of moral development were the villains? the heroes? Did any characters show changes in moral maturity during the story? If so, what caused the changes?

Personal Reflection

1. The most important ideas that I learned in this chapter were

2. This chapter made me think about

3. I would like to find out more about

4. What do you think are the best ideas and the biggest weaknesses in each of the models of moral development presented in this chapter?

5. List three people whose ethical character and integrity you most look up to and whom you admire. What do you see in each person that you would most like to develop in your life?

6. Do you think the differences in the Justice Model and the Caring Model are really the only differences between how men and women think about ethics? Do you think there might be other differences that were not discussed in this chapter? Explain your answer.

4 Critical Thinking in Ethics

Chapter Goals

After completing this chapter, you should be able to:

■ Describe and identify common fallacies in reasoning.

■ Explain and apply the ETHICS model to make ethical decisions based on sound critical-thinking skills.

Key Terms & Concepts

critical thinking

logical fallacies

inconsistency

two-wrongs-make-a-right

either/or

is/ought

red herring

hasty generalization

post hoc

slippery slope

questionable claim

provincialism

false appeal to authority

false appeal to popularity

ETHICS model

stakeholders

justification

What do you think?

Alicia works for a company that makes parts for computers. She has worked in the production department for four years, receiving strong evaluations and praise from her supervisors. She has just learned that she did not get a promotion she had been hoping for. Instead, Clark, a nephew of the company president, is promoted. Clark has worked at the company for two years. The general consensus among the employees is that he is not especially talented and doesn't work any harder than he has to. Alicia meets with her current supervisor, Maria, to protest the decision.

Maria: I know you're upset, Alicia. But relatives of administrators tend to be first in line for promotions. That's the way we've always handled promotions here, so it must be right.

Alicia: But you don't understand! If I don't get this promotion, I can't make my car payments. If I lose my car, I can't get to work. Then I'll lose my job. Without my job, I won't be able to pay my rent. I'll be penniless and homeless on the streets!

Maria: I think you're overreacting. You young people are always overreacting about things.

Alicia: Well, don't you think the person who works the hardest and does the best job should get the promotions?

Maria: My, those are lovely shoes you're wearing. Did you find them at the outlet mall?

Alicia: Don't try to change the subject. What happened here isn't fair, and I'm angry! Wouldn't you think it was wrong if the company gave your job to a less talented goof-off just because he or she was a relative of an executive?

Maria: Yes, but it's different with me. I work very hard.

Alicia: This is impossible! The cook in the lunchroom agreed that I should have gotten the promotion. Go ask him yourself!

Do the statements by Maria and Alicia make logical sense? How would you know? What tools can you use to test whether a statement makes logical sense?

Educators have been talking about the term *critical thinking* for many years. It's a concept that is easier to understand than to do. **Critical thinking** is the process of logical problem solving. People use critical-thinking skills in math to resolve mathematics problems, in science to resolve scientific problems, and in ethics to resolve ethical and moral problems. The goal in ethics is for a person to utilize sound critical-thinking skills so that his or her opinions about ethical issues are logical and well-founded.

You Decide

Analyze the following statements. For each statement, decide whether you think it makes logical sense. (This is *not* the same as deciding whether you agree with the statement.) If you think the statement makes logical sense, explain why. If you don't think the statement makes logical sense, describe any problems in logic that you find.

1. Adults are all alike! They are never satisfied with anything you do!

_____

_____

2. Either you join the protest against the death penalty or you don't respect human life.

_____

_____

3. Most elementary school teachers agree that physical education classes are important to a child's growth and development; therefore, it must be true.

_____

_____

4. I'll never go on another cruise. My family went on a cruise when I was ten. A month later my parents decided to get a divorce. Cruises are bad news!

_____

_____

5. Yes, I cheated on the exam. But you shouldn't fail me because Clara turned in a paper she bought off the Internet!

_____

_____

Personal Reflection

Briefly describe a time when you argued with someone (or listened to people argue) about a controversial issue or question. What was the argument about? What emotions do you remember experiencing (confusion? frustration? anger?). Did either person end up changing his or her opinion? If so, who, how, and why?

"We only think when we are confronted with a problem."

—John Dewey

Logical Fallacies and Ethical Reasoning

The desire to have others agree with one's opinions seems to be a part of human nature. So a discussion with a friend over a difference of opinion usually involves each person sharing and arguing his or her own point of view. However, your main goal as a critical thinker is not so much to win arguments as it is to seek truth—that is, to find the best answers to life's questions and problems. To achieve that, you need to acknowledge strengths in the arguments of others and admit any weaknesses in your own. If your friend's arguments are stronger than your arguments, you haven't lost a contest; you've learned something new. Unfortunately, at times, your pride may get in the way of your learning. You may fear that if you lose an argument, you will appear to be weak. You stop looking for the best possible answers and start trying to win the argument at all costs. In doing so, you may resort to the use of fallacies.

Logical fallacies are illogical or deceptive arguments. Ideally, your arguments should appeal to other people's intellects. Fallacies, however, are often aimed at people's emotions. Fallacies are often based on ignorance, but are sometimes utilized to manipulate or trick others into agreeing with you. You may win some arguments, but you are not likely to find the best answers to your questions. Therefore, critical thinking in ethics includes trying to avoid the use of fallacies in arguments and noticing fallacies present in arguments made by others. To do that, you need to understand what some of those fallacies are. Philosophers have identified over 120 logical fallacies! You'll be relieved to know that you won't be learning about all of them, but the following fallacies are commonly used in ethical discussions. (See Illustration 4-1.)

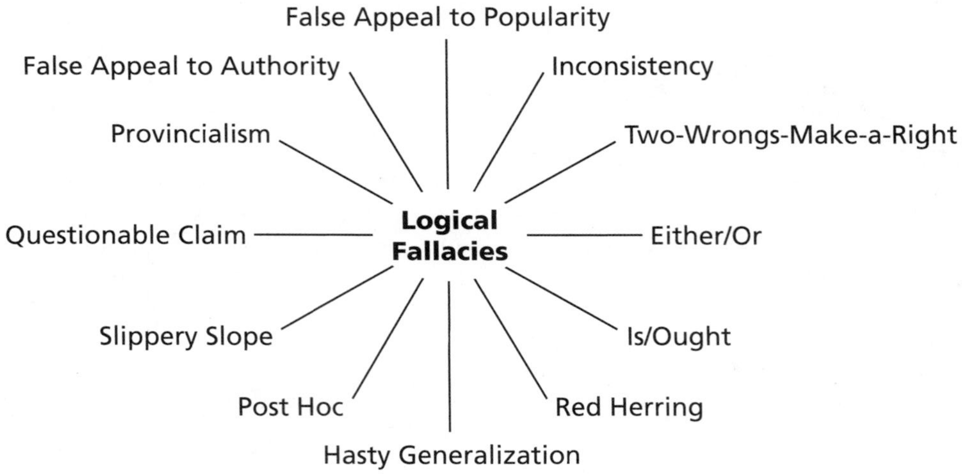

Illustration 4-1

"When you know a thing, to hold that you know it; and when you do not know a thing, to hold that you do not know it: this is knowledge."

—Confucius

Inconsistency

Inconsistency is the fallacy of contradicting oneself in words or actions without being able to logically defend the contradictions. It is the error of saying one thing while doing the opposite or of saying two things that contradict each other. For example, a father regularly lectures his child about the importance of honesty, but acts dishonestly himself. Or a teenage girl tells her Friday night date that she will love only him forever, then says the same words to a different boy on Saturday.

Two-Wrongs-Make-a-Right

Two-wrongs-make-a-right is the fallacy of defending a wrong act by pointing out that someone else did it, too. A young child, about to be punished for coloring on a wall, protests, "Well, Susie did it first!" And what do people often say (or at least think) when a police officer pulls them over for driving too fast? "Yes, officer, I was going over the speed limit. But you should have seen that car that just passed me! It was really flying!" Obviously, a person's wrong actions do not become acceptable just because other people do them, too.

Either/Or

Either/or is the fallacy of making it appear that there are only two possible sides to an issue, one good and one bad. This fallacy is an attempt to make other people think that they are in some kind of a logical trap when, in fact, the trap does not exist. A coach may tell an athlete that unless the athlete takes illegal steroids or plays injured, he or she has no commitment to the team. Someone at school may say, "Either do drugs with us, or you aren't cool." Real-life situations usually involve more than two choices.

Is/Ought

Is/ought is the fallacy of stating that because things are a certain way now, they should remain that way. In other words, whatever *is* now *ought* to be that way always, so nothing should change. This fallacy is often used by people who fear change. A famous example of the is/ought fallacy was used to warn against the invention of the airplane. Skeptics said, "If people were meant to fly, they'd have wings." In other words, "People are earthbound now, so that is how they should remain." Today similar arguments are used against adopting new forms of technology—from experimenting in genetics to expanding the role of computers in society. Some people see change as frightening and find security in keeping things the way they are.

Red Herring

Red herring is the fallacy of using an unrelated idea in an argument to distract your opponent. It is said that the name came from a once common practice in English fox hunting. To get the hounds to stop chasing the fox, the hunters would drag a smoked fish across the fox's trail. The dogs, charging down the path, would be diverted by the stronger, more interesting scent. The red herring fallacy accomplishes the same goal by using interesting but irrelevant arguments. For example, a teen complains that a parent is consistently late in picking him up after school. The parent responds by scolding the teen for not keeping his room clean. Do you see the attempt at distraction? A store owner catches someone shoplifting. When the police arrive, the thief complains that the merchandise was overpriced.

Hasty Generalization

Hasty generalization is the fallacy of assuming that most members of a group share a common characteristic, when this assumption is actually based on only a few observations. For example, because two left-handed people spoke harshly to Mitsu, she wrongly assumed that left-handers as a group are irritable people. Many of the unfair stereotypes and prejudices that a person has about other groups of people are based on hasty generalizations. These stereotypes often start with people being taught a faulty belief about some other group. Perhaps Mitsu grew up hearing that left-handed people are irritable. Then when she experienced a few people from the group acting that way, her belief was reinforced. As a result, people come to believe such stereotypes are true, based on only a few examples.

Post Hoc

Post hoc is the fallacy of assuming that because two events happened in a short period of time, the first action must have caused the second action. People's minds interpret events this way so people can make sense of what they see around them. So when they see events that occur one after the other, their minds sometimes assume that one event caused the other. But this assumption is not always accurate and can lead to some funny mistakes. Many superstitions and myths are a result of post hoc fallacies. For example, "A black cat crossed my path on Tuesday; then on Wednesday, my car was hit by a bus. That proves black cats are bad luck!" Wouldn't you like to know what happened to the person who started the superstition that walking under a ladder causes bad luck? Sometimes one event or action does cause another, but not always. Many times, what looks like a cause is really a coincidence.

Slippery Slope

The **slippery slope** fallacy is an attempt to frighten others into rejecting an idea by trying to show that accepting it would start a chain reaction of terrible events. This chain reaction often involves a series of steps that keep getting worse. At the end of the chain reaction is a terrifying or ridiculous consequence that no rational person would want. Consider the following example of a slippery slope used to explain why a law banning assault rifles should not be passed. Notice that the steps continue to get worse. Would passing the law automatically lead to the final result?

Sure, all the government says it wants to do now is to ban deadly assault rifles. But the next thing you know it will try to prevent citizens from owning any kind of handgun, then it will take away hunting rifles, then shotguns. Eventually, kids will be going to prison for having BB guns and water pistols! We can stop this lunacy by voting to protect people's access to deadly assault rifles!

Questionable Claim

Questionable claim is the fallacy of using statements that are too broad or too exaggerated to be true. Words such as *all, every, never,* and *none* are often used in questionable claim statements. Examples include all *athletes are dumb,* every *pit bull is vicious, or teachers* never *care about how students feel.* As you can see, disproving a questionable claim fallacy requires only one exception.

Ethics & Law

As stated earlier, your main goal as an ethical thinker is to find truth—or at least the best answers you can find to your problems. However, that isn't always the case. The goal of an attorney arguing a case is to win the argument, not necessarily to find the truth. Thus, attorneys are sometimes put in the position of arguing points that they don't personally believe. There are some limits, though. For example, lawyers are not allowed to lie or to put someone on the stand who they know will lie. But that still leaves ethical dilemmas such as an attorney zealously arguing for a criminal defendant that the attorney strongly suspects is guilty. Would you be able to justify those actions to yourself if you were an attorney?

Provincialism

Provincialism is the fallacy of looking at an issue or a question from your point of view or from the point of view of people like you. It is a fallacy of narrow-mindedness, of not trying to see the viewpoints of others. For example, Rosario, a wealthy person, argues against taxing the rich to provide social programs for the underprivileged. She doesn't care that those programs help many people live better lives. All that matters to her are the effects of the programs on people like her.

This fallacy is an easy trap to fall into because the first tool that many people have in interpreting the world around them is their own point of view. However, most people also use *empathy*, the skill of understanding the feelings and perspectives of others. A person using the provincialism fallacy does not have the ability to use empathy or simply chooses not to empathize.

False Appeal to Authority

False appeal to authority is the fallacy of incorrectly relying on authority figures or experts to support your argument. It is not always a fallacy to rely on authority figures to back up your point of view. After all, that is one purpose of research. But the authorities referred to should be real experts and have some special insight into the issue being discussed. The fallacy occurs when your expert is not an authority in the area you are talking about or when other experts seem to agree that your expert is wrong. For example, if you want to convince a friend that using animals in medical experiments is not always morally wrong, it would not be appropriate for you to quote a famous movie star who happens to agree with your opinion. All by itself, having a famous name does not make anyone an authority. A more appropriate expert on using animals for experiments would be a doctor or a scientist.

False Appeal to Popularity

False appeal to popularity is the fallacy of assuming that an idea is right because many people believe it is right. People using this fallacy believe that if an idea is popular, it must be true. Do you know people who often base their opinions on what others think? Consider this example: A student in an ethics class stated that he was in favor of the death penalty because he had read in the newspaper that 82 percent of Americans were for it. He asked, "How could that many people be wrong?" Powerful arguments exist on both sides of the death penalty issue, but relying on popularity alone is not one of them. At different times in history, a majority of humans have believed that the earth was flat; that it was the center of the universe; and that the stars were small holes in the night sky, letting in light from the other side. No idea becomes true just because it is popular.

Checkpoint

In your own words, summarize the meanings of each of these logical fallacies.

inconsistency: _____

_____

_____

two-wrongs-make-a-right: _____

_____

_____

either/or: _____

_____

_____

is/ought: _____

_____

_____

red herring: _____

_____

_____

hasty generalization: _____

_____

_____

post hoc: _____

_____

_____

slippery slope: _____

_____

_____

questionable claim: _____

_____

_____

provincialism: _____

_____

_____

false appeal to authority: _____

_____

false appeal to popularity: _____

_____

_____

The following fallacies are included in the scenario at the beginning of the chapter. Locate each fallacy and write the phrase in which it is used.

- false appeal to authority

_____

_____

_____

- questionable claim

_____

_____

_____

- slippery slope

_____

_____

_____

- red herring

_____

_____

_____

- is/ought

_____

_____

_____

- inconsistency

_____

_____

_____

Personal Reflection

1. Three logical fallacies that I hear others using most often are

2. Three logical fallacies that I hear myself using most often are

3. One way that understanding these fallacies can help me in discussions with others is

Real-World Ethics

©Getty Images/PhotoDisc

According to a recent study conducted by three major research universities, children and teens are demonstrating poor sportsmanship at surprisingly high levels. 803 youth athletes, ages 9–15, were surveyed. Among the study's findings:

- 10% of the athletes admitted to cheating in their sport.
- 13% said they had intentionally tried to injure an opponent.
- 13% admitted to making fun of less-skilled teammates.
- 27% said they had acted like "bad sports."
- 31% admitted to arguing with officials.

As stated earlier, critical thinking is primarily a problem-solving process. It requires open-minded, consistent, and creative reasoning. Critical thinking in ethics is more than an attitude or a state of mind. It is made up of several specific skills that almost anyone can learn. In fact, you have already practiced using the skills in this chapter and in earlier chapters. Now it is time to put the skills together to create a model for finding your own answers to ethical questions.

The ETHICS Model

The **ETHICS model** is a structured approach to making ethical decisions. It was created by Mary Dawn Pyle, a professor at St. Petersburg College's Applied Ethics Program. Writers and teachers have proposed many similar decision-making models, but the ETHICS model is simple to learn and remember, while having enough depth to allow for the complex ethical dilemmas that people face in life.

The ETHICS model is composed of six steps that can help people make better ethical decisions. The first letter of the first word in each step spells out the word *ethics*.

Evaluate the Problem

Start with the big picture, taking in all of the details and complexities of the situation. Then begin analyzing the information, gradually narrowing down the scope until you identify the central ethical decision you must make. For example, if a store employee sees a coworker stealing, the central ethical decision may be *what should the employee do about what he or she witnessed?* If a teen has a friend who is drinking often, the central ethical decision is *what should the teen do about the friend's drinking problem?* If a student has direct knowledge that a teacher at school is doing something illegal, the central ethical decision is *what should the student do about what he or she knows?*

The "what should ____ do?" format is important because the ultimate goal of the ETHICS model is to determine the wisest and most ethical course of action. If the question is not framed properly, the answer will be more difficult to find.

Think Through the Options

The next step is to consider what options are available to the decision maker. It is very important to consider as many options as possible. For some reason, people often have a tendency to think of ethical decisions in either/or terms.

- Either I tell on the stealing coworker or I don't.
- Either I confront my friend's drinking problem or I ignore it.
- Either I report the teacher or I keep quiet.

In reality, the decisions that a person faces in life present an almost infinite number of options. The key is creativity. What options are available to the employee who witnessed the theft?

- Ignore the thefts.
- Join the thief in stealing merchandise.
- Research company policy about employee theft to determine whether other employees have a duty to report it.
- Report the coworker's actions to a supervisor.
- Report the thefts anonymously.
- Confront the coworker privately with an ultimatum that the next theft will be reported.
- Gather several other employees to confront the coworker as a group.
- Ask a more experienced (and honest) coworker for advice.

You may not be comfortable with some of those options, but note that it was not difficult to identify eight possible responses. The goal is to list as many as possible. The more creative you are in listing responses, the stronger your final decision is likely to be.

"No one is ever so wrong as the man who knows all the answers."

—Thomas Merton

Highlight the Stakeholders

Stakeholders are the people or groups of people who might be affected by a specific decision. They have a stake in the decision because the consequences may affect them. It is important to include as many stakeholders as possible in this step. Consider the student who has knowledge of a teacher's illegal activity. Who are the stakeholders?

- The inappropriate teacher
- The teacher's family
- The student
- The student's family
- The student's friends
- School administrators and the school district
- Other teachers at the school (and elsewhere)
- Other students at the school
- Parents of other students at the school
- Other students whom this teacher might endanger in the future
- Community leaders
- Members of the community at large

The consequences of ethical and unethical actions are like ripples on a pond. They may affect only a few people at first, but they often spread wider to include many more people than originally anticipated. The more stakeholders you consider at this stage, the more balanced and fair your final decision will be.

Learn More

Search the Internet to find useful information about critical thinking, decision making, or ethical decision making. Select one web site and write a one-page summary/reaction report of what you find. Bring the paper to class for discussion.

Identify and Apply Relevant Ethical Principles

This step is the heart of the ETHICS model. The goal is not just to make a decision, but to make an ethical decision. And the universal ethical principles that were discussed in Chapter 2 are the keys. As a quick review, those principles are as follows:

- **Egoism Principle:** The right thing for a person to do in any situation is the action that best serves that person's own long-term interests.
- **Utility Principle:** The morally right action is the one that produces the best consequences for everyone involved, not just for one individual.
- **Principle of Rights:** An action is considered moral when it respects the rights of others and is considered immoral when it violates another's rights.
- **Principle of Duties:** People should do what is ethically right purely because people have a moral obligation to do what is ethically right. They should do the right thing because it's the right thing to do.
- **Principle of Virtues:** Ethics is based on being a good person, that is, on incorporating ideal character traits into your life.

So how do you go about applying those principles to the central ethical decision to be made? You simply look at the situation from each principle's perspective. What would each principle imply as the most ethical course of action?

Consider again the situation of the employee who witnessed a coworker stealing from the store. Based on each principle, what should the witnessing employee do? The following chart answers that question.

Principle	Application
Egoism	The witnessing employee should do whatever is in his or her long-term best interest. Reporting the thefts would impress company managers and might lead to a reward. On the other hand, not reporting the thefts could serve the witnessing employee's self-interest (for example, blackmailing the coworker).
Utility	What action would produce the most overall happiness for the most people? The answer to that question depends largely on the situation. If the thefts are significant, they are affecting many people. Other employees may be under suspicion, and money that could have gone toward increases in employee pay may be spent on security instead. Customers may be paying higher prices to make up for the lost profits. Reporting the thefts would likely be the best choice here.
Rights	The thief is clearly violating the rights of others and, therefore, forfeiting any rights he or she might have in expecting loyalty from coworkers. Reporting the thefts does not violate anyone's rights. Not reporting them would violate the rights of the store owners, honest employees, and perhaps the customers.
Duties	This is the duty to do the right thing, no matter what. So what's the right thing to do? Somehow you already know, don't you? If someone was stealing from the witnessing employee, the employee would want others to report what they knew and put an end to the stealing. Therefore, that is what the employee should do now.
Virtues	What ethical virtues apply to situations like this? Honesty, integrity, trustworthiness, courage, and fairness, among others. All of those virtues seem to suggest that the witnessing employee should report the thefts.

Remember that principles may apply better to some ethical questions and situations than others. And different principles sometimes conflict with one another. So the process is not as simple as completing a yes/no checklist. When most of the principles end up suggesting the same course of action, as in the preceding example, the decision maker can have some measure of confidence that a particular option is a good moral choice.

Choose the Wisest Option

This is where you put it all together. Go back and review the first four steps in the ETHICS model.

- What central ethical decision had to be made in the situation or scenario?
- What options were listed?
  - Do some options seem to represent better ethical actions?
  - Can any options be eliminated from consideration as ethical courses of actions?
- What stakeholders were identified?
  - How are the stakeholders affected?
  - Are any options clearly unfair and harmful to one or more stakeholders?
  - Do any options seem to benefit most or all of the stakeholders?
- How did the ethical principles apply?
  - Did any options clearly violate one or more of the principles?
  - Is this a situation in which self-interest should be sacrificed for the greater good?
  - Is this a situation in which the greater good should be sacrificed to protect individual rights?
  - Did most of the principles seem to favor one option?

After careful consideration of all of the relevant factors, choose the option that seems to represent the wisest and most ethical course of action.

State Your Justification

Justification refers to the reasons and arguments that support a decision. Ethical decisions are often controversial. It is likely that at least some other people will not agree with your decision. Therefore, you may need to explain and defend your decision.

A strength of the ETHICS model is that you have already considered, and perhaps documented, much of the information that you need. Your justification lies in the process you went through in making your decision. You can rely on information from any and all of the steps in the model.

How strong the justification needs to be depends on how strong the opposition is to the decision. Some decisions result in many rounds of pro and con arguments, but those decisions are not the norm. A good rule of thumb is to be able to provide three to five strong reasons or arguments that support the decision made.

Checkpoint

Briefly explain each step in the ETHICS model of ethical decision making.

E: _____

T: _____

H: _____

I: _____

C: _____

S: _____

What do you think now?

Consider the scenario about Alicia at the beginning of the chapter. Assume that the company president knew that Alicia was a better worker than Clark but gave the promotion to Clark anyway. Review the ethical principles discussed in the I step of the ETHICS model. Using those principles, decide whether it was right or wrong for the president to give Clark the promotion.

_____

_____

_____

_____

Personal Reflection

Think of an ethical decision that you had to make recently or that you are facing now. Apply the ETHICS model to your decision to determine the wisest and most ethical course of action. (You do not have to share these details with anyone unless you choose to do so.)

Evaluate the problem:

Think through the options:

Highlight the stakeholders:

Identify and apply relevant ethical principles:

Choose the wisest option:

State your justification:

Summary

Logical fallacies are inappropriate or deceptive arguments. They are often used from ignorance, but are sometimes utilized to manipulate or trick others into agreeing.

The ETHICS model is a six-step structured approach to making ethical decisions. The six steps are evaluate the problem; think through the options; highlight the stakeholders; identify and apply relevant ethical principles; choose the wisest, most ethical option; and state your justification.

Vocabulary Builder

Match the following terms to their definitions.

a. critical thinking

b. either/or

c. ETHICS model

d. false appeal to authority

e. false appeal to popularity

f. hasty generalization

g. inconsistency

h. is/ought

i. justification

j. logical fallacies

k. post hoc

l. provincialism

m. questionable claim

n. red herring

o. slippery slope

p. stakeholders

q. two-wrongs-make-a-right

1. _____ An attempt to frighten others into rejecting an idea by trying to show that accepting it would start a chain reaction of terrible events.

2. _____ Illogical or deceptive arguments.

3. _____ The fallacy of assuming that an idea is right because many people believe it is right.

4. _____ The fallacy of assuming that because two events happened in a short period of time, the first action must have caused the second action.

5. _____ The fallacy of assuming that most members of a group share a common characteristic, when this assumption is actually based on only a few observations.

6. _____ The fallacy of contradicting oneself in words or actions without being able to logically defend the contradictions.

7. _____ The fallacy of defending a wrong act by pointing out that someone else did it, too.

8. _____ The fallacy of incorrectly relying on authority figures or experts to support an argument.

9. _____ The fallacy of a person looking at an issue or a question from his or her point of view or from the point of view of people like him or her.

10. _____ The fallacy of making it appear that there are only two possible sides to an issue, one good and one bad.

11. _____ The fallacy of stating that because things are a certain way now, they should remain that way.

12. _____ The fallacy of using an unrelated idea in an argument to distract an opponent.

13. _____ The fallacy of using statements that are too broad or too exaggerated to be true.

14. _____ People or groups of people who might be affected by a specific decision.

15. _____ The process of logical problem solving.

16. _____ The reasons and arguments that support a decision.

17. _____ A structured approach to making ethical decisions.

Reinforcement

1. Create an original example of each fallacy.

a. inconsistency: _____

_____

b. two-wrongs-make-a-right: _____

_____

c. either/or: _____

_____

d. is/ought: _____

_____

e. red herring: _____

_____

f. hasty generalization: _____

_____

g. post hoc: _____

_____

h. slippery slope: _____

_____

i. questionable claim: _____

_____

j. provincialism: _____

_____

k. false appeal to authority: _____

_____

l. false appeal to popularity: _____

_____

2. Supply the appropriate letter from the ETHICS acronym to the action involved in that step of the model.

_____ Analyze the information to identify the central ethical decision to be made.
_____ Apply universal ethical principles to the central ethical decision to be made.
_____ Consider the people or groups of people who might be affected by a specific decision.
_____ Consider what options are available to the decision maker.
_____ Explain and defend the decision that was made.
_____ Select the option that seems to represent the wisest and most ethical course of action.

Thinking Critically

1. On the blank beside each statement, write the name of the fallacy that best describes it.

a. _____ I think you are wrong about the danger of the sun's ultraviolet rays. After all, look how well our football team has been playing lately!

b. _____ I can't support your idea about reserving the closest parking places for seniors. I don't care about the great things they've done for this school. I'm a sophomore, and on rainy days, I sometimes have to park a half a mile away.

c. _____ Either you sell 100 candy bars for the fund-raiser or you don't really care about our band!

d. _____ If we don't let Luis be the yearbook editor, he might tell his mother, who happens to be the principal. Then she might accuse us of breaking a rule and suspend us. Then we might get behind in school and not graduate on time. Then we might not get accepted into college or technical school. We might never get a job! Let's just let Luis be the editor.

e. _____ It is absolutely wrong for teenagers to use illegal drugs. People should protect their minds and bodies. Relying on drugs is no way to deal with problems. It's just wrong! I do drink a lot of beer, though.

f. _____ Last week I read that an elected city official was arrested for accepting a bribe. Today's paper said that another politician was caught doing the same thing. So I have concluded that all politicians are corrupt and dishonest.

g. _____ I know for a fact that the square root of 16 is 8. I heard it directly from the sportscaster on Channel 8.

h. _____ A tradition at this school is that 11th graders always go to lunch first. That's just the way it is, so that's how it should stay.

i. _____ All blue-eyed people are intelligent.

j. _____ Yes, I spray-painted graffiti on a wall in the gym. But Jerry painted a lot more graffiti than I did. He's the one who should be punished!

k. _____ This morning I had leftover pizza for breakfast. Then I wrecked the driver's education car. Evidently, pizza causes car accidents.

l. _____ In a school survey, 90 percent of students said that they would learn more if school days lasted only two hours. Therefore, it must be true that we need shorter school days.

2. Read the following scenario. Identify any logical fallacies you see in the story. Then apply the ETHICS model to determine the wisest and most ethical course of action.

You have a new job as a salesperson for Integrity Supplies. This work requires you to spend a lot of time on the road, traveling from town to town to sell Integrity's products to businesses. You eat a lot of meals in restaurants and spend a lot of nights in motels. The company reimburses your travel expenses when you turn in your receipts after each trip. You are paid a straight commission, meaning that you get to keep a percentage of each sale. You make a nice commission when you sell a lot, but there are times when you work very hard and make very little.

One day when you are getting ready to turn in your travel receipts, a more experienced coworker pulls you aside to tell you about the practice of "adjusting receipts." Evidently, it is common practice at Integrity for salespeople to make small changes on their receipts, adding a little here and a little there to increase the company reimbursements. The coworker explains, "All of us on the sales staff have done this for years. You just turn 4s and 7s into 9s and 2s into 8s. If you're careful and make several copies of copies, no one can tell the difference."

When you reply that this sounds dishonest, the coworker replies, "Look, we all do it! If you don't go along with the idea, it could make the rest of us look bad. It can get very lonely here for someone who isn't a team player! Maybe 'adjusting the receipts' is a little borderline ethically, but it's not fair that we get paid only when we sell something. We're just trying to make a living, and this helps protect us in the lean times. As far as I know, no one's ever gotten in trouble for it."

What Should You Do?

evaluate the problem: _____

_____

_____

_____

think through the options: _____

_____

_____

_____

highlight the stakeholders: _____

_____

_____

_____

identify and apply relevant ethical principles: _____

_____

_____

_____

choose the wisest option: _____

_____

_____

_____

state your justification: _____

_____

_____

_____

Digging Deeper

1. Go on a "fallacy fishing trip" for a few days. Try to "catch" examples of people using some of the fallacies discussed in this chapter. Good "fallacy fishing holes" may include newspapers, television and radio talk shows, magazine articles about controversial issues, television news shows, and political debates. See who in your class can come back with the most fallacies or the biggest "whoppers."

2. Write a one-page paper arguing for or against some issue. If that sounds boring, consider this: Your goal is to write the absolute *worst* arguments that you possibly can. The trick is to see how many fallacies you can squeeze into one page. Bonus points go to anyone who includes all 12!

3. Do some research (newspapers, magazines, television news shows, and so on) to find an example of someone making poor or unwise ethical and/or legal decisions. Apply the ETHICS model to that situation. Demonstrate where the person's decision-making skills broke down and how the person could have made wiser decisions if he or she had used better critical-thinking skills.

Personal Reflection

1. The most important ideas that I learned in this chapter were

2. This chapter made me think about

3. I would like to find out more about

4. One step I could take toward making better and wiser ethical decisions is

5

Ethics and Advertising

Chapter Goals

After completing this chapter you should be able to:

■ Identify and explain common ethical problems in advertising.

■ Describe ethical standards of the advertising profession.

Key Terms & Concepts

advertising	telemarketing	guarantee
false advertising	code of ethics	warranty
puffery	substantiation	testimonial
bait and switch		

What do you think?

Sam owns a small advertising company. He specializes in creating print ads for area magazines and newspapers. His clients are primarily small to medium-sized retail businesses. Sam makes a decent living, but with only four employees, he is not getting rich. Still, he enjoys the creative process, making his customers happy, and seeing his creations in print.

One day a representative from a national fast-food chain calls to request Sam's services. The representative has seen some of Sam's ads and is impressed. She wants to hire Sam's firm to create some regional print ads, and she suggests the possibility of a national ad campaign if things go well. For Sam, it is the opportunity of a lifetime. Almost overnight his small firm will garner national attention. He will be able to hire more staff and may be able to attract other national corporations if he does a good job with the campaign.

Everything goes smoothly until Sam's first meeting with the company's advertising staff. As they are discussing the general themes of the ad campaign, Sam states in passing that he is grateful to be working with a corporation of such integrity. He mentions company materials describing the firm's dedication to producing "top-quality foods that promote the health of our customers." One of the company's employees gives a short laugh and says that Sam shouldn't put too much faith in the company's brochures. "Let's just say that our food probably won't hurt you if you're living a healthy lifestyle, but I wouldn't go much farther than that." When Sam presses the group, someone admits that the company's health claims are unproven and most likely exaggerated.

Sam considers the situation later in the day. This campaign is his chance, maybe his only chance, to make it big in the advertising world. But he knows that the company will insist on including its health claims in the ads—claims that he now knows are untrue. He would be a party to deceiving the public and perhaps harming people. On the other hand, he tells himself, advertisers aren't really responsible for the false claims of their clients.

What do you think?

In the 1990 movie *Crazy People*, actor Dudley Moore played the role of an advertising executive who, suffering from an attack of conscience, resolved to create only truthful ads. Examples of his honest ads included the following:

Automobiles:	"They're boxy, but they're good. And in these dangerous times, isn't safe more important than sexy?"
Airline:	"Most of our passengers get there alive."
Cigarettes:	"Pulmonary cancer, maybe. Flavor, for sure."
Travel:	"The French can be annoying. Come to Greece; we're nicer."
Life insurance:	"We know you love him. But if he happens to die, we'll give you two Mercedes and a summer home. Wouldn't that be nice, too?"

The ad executive's employers promptly concluded that he had lost his mind and put him in a mental institution. In the words of one coworker: "We can't level with people; we're in advertising!"

Advertising is the practice of attracting public attention to a product or business for the purpose of increasing sales. Contrary to the implications in *Crazy People*, most people in the field of advertising act ethically and serve an essential function in business. How can people purchase a product if they don't know about it? On the other hand, there is a fine line between encouraging people to buy a car and manipulating or deceiving people into buying a car. What constitutes ethics in advertising?

You Decide

Analyze the following hypothetical advertisements. Decide whether you think each example contains an ethical problem. If you think there is an ethical problem, explain what it is. If you don't think there is an ethical problem, explain why.

1. Television commercials for "Flying Man" action figures. The commercials, which run each Saturday morning during the "Flying Man" cartoon, show the toys flying, although small print on the screen states that they don't actually fly.

_____

_____

_____

2. An ad for plastic surgery in a popular magazine for teenage girls.

_____

_____

_____

3. An advertisement for a dance studio, in a magazine for senior citizens. The ad highlights several benefits of dance lessons, including companionship, improved health, and relief from loneliness.

_____

_____

_____

4. Beer commercials that air during prime time on a popular cable TV music video channel.

_____

_____

_____

5. Television and print commercials for a bank that issues credit cards, advertising a 0 percent interest rate for the first six months. No mention is made of what happens to the interest rates after that time.

_____

_____

_____

Personal Reflection

Briefly describe a time when you were duped by a misleading advertisement and ended up with something less than the ad led you to believe. How did the experience make you feel?

Ethical Problems in Advertising

People don't tend to think of false advertising as being as serious as, say, environmental destruction or discrimination. However, dishonest advertising and marketing do cause harm to individuals through manipulation and exploitation. Keep that thought in mind as you read about several important ethical issues in advertising.

False Advertising

Sellers sometimes lie. **False advertising** is the practice of making statements about products that the advertiser knows are not true. The claims can be about how the product works, how it is made, or how it will affect people who buy or use it. In the early and mid-1900s, tobacco companies lied to the public regularly about cigarettes. The tobacco companies claimed that their cigarettes were healthier than their competitors' brands, often citing research done by scientists they employed. They even made the claim that some cigarette brands were good for people!

Besides being unethical and dishonest, false advertising isn't even smart—at least in the long run. Consumers eventually figure out the truth, and the public's backlash can be severe. Many of the tobacco companies lost millions of dollars in lawsuits filed by former customers (or their families) who contracted cancer from smoking the "healthy" cigarettes. In a society where lawsuits are common, false and deceptive advertising is unwise and expensive.

Puffery

Puffery is the term used to describe statements that are not outright lies, but merely exaggerations. Is anything wrong with a chewing gum claiming to be "the best taste your mouth ever had" or an amusement park claiming to be "the best time you'll ever have in one day"? After trying the products, some people might actually agree with the statements; however, others would not. But is puffery unethical? Should puffery claims be illegal?

The Federal Trade Commission (FTC) is charged with regulating advertising and advertisers. The FTC allows puffery, defining it as claims (1) that reasonable people do not believe to be true product qualities and (2) that are incapable of being proven either true or false. Some consumer groups have criticized the FTC for allowing deceptive claims through this loophole of puffery.

Bait and Switch

An appliance store places a newspaper advertisement offering a top-of-the-line refrigerator for $200. The next morning lines start forming early and continue to lengthen. By the time the store opens, hundreds of customers are lined up to take advantage of the offer. But the advantage turns out to belong to the store. It has only ten of that particular model in stock, and those refrigerators are gone in minutes. The vast majority of the customers find only apologetic salespeople offering to show them other refrigerators that cost much more.

Bait and switch is the practice of advertising a product at a low price while intentionally stocking only a limited number in hopes of luring shoppers to buy more expensive items. This practice is illegal, but can sometimes be difficult to prove. Generally, there is no legally mandated minimum number of products that must be kept in stock. However, businesses that advertise discounted prices on a product in short supply are usually required to do one of the following:

- Clearly state the number of the products in stock.
- Offer rain checks to customers who request them. Rain checks are written guarantees that customers can have the product at the discounted price when more are delivered to the store.

Advertising to Children

Children are especially vulnerable to deceptive advertising. They are generally trusting and believe what adults tell them. Children tend to be naïve, often believing that claims on TV or in the newspaper are true (a quality shared by many adults, as well). In addition, children often have difficulty differentiating between fantasy and reality. If a superhero can become invisible in a cartoon, children are likely to believe that the action figure will do the same once it is in their home.

Because of children's vulnerabilities, laws have been passed to protect children from deception and manipulation. One such law prohibits creators and producers of a children's cartoon from advertising products related to the characters of that program during the broadcast. However, a child's best defense is involved, attentive family members who can help the child understand what is true and real.

Telemarketing

Telemarketing is the practice of selling directly to individuals through unsolicited phone calls, e-mails, or faxes. Innovations in technology have made this practice more common. Computers can dial hundreds of phones, send out thousands of faxes, and deliver millions of unwanted spam (electronic junk mail). Meanwhile, customers are often left feeling frustrated and powerless to stop the deluge. Many customers believe that the telemarketers are wasting their time. Worse still, the unsolicited ads waste customers' money (through use of paper, toner, and minutes on cell phones). Telemarketers make very little money per call, e-mail, or fax, but so many ads are sent out that a few eventually result in sales.

Political leaders have noticed the growing sense of frustration—even outrage—by the general public. Laws have been passed allowing people to sign up for "do not call" lists. Telemarketing firms that continue to send unsolicited ads to people on the lists can face fines or other sanctions. Senders of spam are supposed to allow people the option of removing their e-mail addresses from the sales list. In addition, some states prohibit the use of automatic calling programs. It seems illogical for sellers to intentionally advertise in ways that alienate potential customers, but telemarketing practices remain lucrative, allowing them to grow.

Ethics & Law

The FTC regulates advertising in the United States. According to the FTC's Deception Policy Statement (1983), an advertisement is considered deceptive (and illegal) based on the following criteria.

1. *The advertisement contains a representation, omission, or practice that is likely to mislead the customer.* This also includes products that do not work as claimed, bait-and-switch advertisements for products not in stock, and failure to fulfill warranty obligations.

2. *The act or practice must be considered from the perspective of the reasonable consumer.* For example, a commercial shows a customer floating with joy in the air after buying a car. A reasonable person is not likely to conclude that purchasing the product would enable him or her to fly. However, a reasonable person might be misled by deceptive claims about gas mileage.

3. *The representation, omission, or practice must be material.* This means that the misrepresentation or practice is likely to affect a consumer's decision to buy a product. It is information that is important to consumers.

"Advertise-ments contain the only truths to be relied on in a newspaper."

—Thomas Jefferson

Checkpoint

1. In your own words, explain each of these ethical issues or concerns in advertising.

a. false advertising _____

_____

b. puffery _____

_____

c. bait and switch _____
_____

d. advertising to children _____
_____

e. telemarketing _____

2. In your own words, explain the three criteria the FTC uses to determine whether an advertisement is deceptive.

_____
_____
_____
_____

What do you think now?

Imagine that Sam, from the small advertising company, came to you for advice about his situation. What ethical issues do you see in his story? What would you advise him to do?

_____
_____
_____
_____

Personal Reflection

Imagine that you own an advertising company. Choose one of the five ethical problems in advertising and explain your company policies pertaining to that issue.

Real-World Ethics

It is becoming common for special interest groups to organize boycotts against companies that place advertisements on certain television shows. In other words, if a group believes that a television program contains content that they disagree with or that they find offensive, the group may tell its members not to buy products from any sponsors of the program. If the group is large and powerful enough, the sponsors may see their profits fall. Defenders of the practice claim that their members have the right to do business with companies that share their values. Others have criticized the practice as manipulative, even referring to it as economic blackmail. What do you think?

©CORBIS

"Good products can be sold by honest advertising. If you don't think the product is good, you have no business to be advertising it."

—David Ogilvy

As mentioned earlier, most people in the field of advertising act professionally and do not resort to unethical tactics. As professionals, they have a vested interest in setting, promoting, and maintaining high ethical standards for themselves and their peers. Members of a professional organization generally publish these standards in a **code of ethics**, a written set of principles and rules intended to serve as a guideline for ethical behavior for individuals under the organization's authority.

The Ethical Standard

The American Advertising Federation (AAF) authored *Advertising Ethics and Principles* in 1984. This code, defined in the following sections, sets the professional standard and provides a way to evaluate the ethics of advertisers.*

Truth

Advertising shall tell the truth, and shall reveal significant facts, the omission of which would mislead the public.

Ethics generally starts with truth and fairness. In the case of advertising, truth and fairness go hand in hand. Lying about a product is unfair to customers who are cheated and exploited by the dishonest claim. So the foundation of ethical advertising is that ads should tell the truth.

Notice the two parts of this principle. All statements made should be truthful, of course. But there is more to honesty than just truthfulness, isn't there? Imagine that you saw an ad for a new car. The ad told you of many wonderful qualities of the car but neglected to mention that the wheels tend to fall off when the driver makes sharp turns. That's a need-to-know fact, isn't it? Intentionally choosing not to reveal important facts about a product is a form of dishonesty, too.

Source: American Advertising Federation (www.aaf.org).

Substantiation

Advertising claims shall be substantiated by evidence in possession of the advertiser and advertising agency, prior to making such claims.

An advertisement for a pain reliever claims that the product relieves twice as much pain as competing products in half the time. Suffering from a headache, you go to the pharmacy and buy a bottle of these wonder pills. After a couple of doses, you come to believe that the claims were not true. This particular pain reliever works about the same as other products you have taken for headaches. So you call the company's consumer hotline and complain. The representative's reply is that the claims were not false advertising because the company believed they might be true. Granted, the company did not have any evidence to support the claims, but its intentions were good.

Ethical advertising requires more than believing that a claim might be true. **Substantiation** is the validation of advertising claims with objective data from independent research. The burden of responsibility is on the advertiser to be able to prove that all claims are true.

Comparisons

Advertising shall refrain from making false, misleading, or unsubstantiated statements or claims about a competitor or his/her products or services.

You live in a small town that has two roofing companies—Bill's Roofing and Jill's Roofing. One day you see a newspaper ad for Bill's that is full of negative statements about Jill's.

- Jill uses inferior nails!
- Jill's shingles aren't waterproof!
- Jill's employees steal lawn furniture!

What would your reaction be? Your first instinct might be to wonder about Jill's business sense or sanity. But what would you think if none of those allegations turned out to be true? Then Bill would be the one in trouble.

To make false claims and comparisons about competitors is unprofessional and unethical, but it is also illegal and unwise. A firm making such claims may be sued for libel.

Bait Advertising

Advertising shall not offer products or services for sale unless such offer constitutes a bona fide effort to sell the advertising products or services and is not a device to switch consumers to other goods or services, usually higher priced.

One trait of an effective code of ethics is that it covers all important ethical issues that arise in the field. You have already read about the unethical advertising practice called *bait and switch*. This provision in the code of ethics forbids such actions.

Guarantees and Warranties

Advertising of guarantees and warranties shall be explicit, with sufficient information to apprise consumers of their principal terms and limitations or, when space or time restrictions preclude such disclosures, the advertisement should clearly reveal where the full text of the guarantee or warranty can be examined before purchase.

Learn More

Use the Internet to research *ethics in advertising* or *unethical advertising*. Choose one interesting web site and share your findings with the class.

After weeks of searching, you bought your first car. It was a used car, but only a few years old. One reason you bought it with confidence was that the dealer offered a bumper-to-bumper warranty. The salesperson promised that if anything went wrong or broke during the first year, the dealer would make the repair at no charge.

Only a couple of weeks after you bought the car, two items broke—the cup holder snapped off, and the rear-window brake light went out. When you took the car back to the dealer for repairs, you were told that those particular items were not covered under the bumper-to-bumper warranty. The cup holder was considered an accessory item, and the lightbulb was considered a regular maintenance item. You left the dealer $117 poorer, feeling disappointed and cheated.

A **guarantee** is an assurance attesting to the durability or quality of a service or product. A **warranty** is a written promise to repair or replace a product if it breaks or becomes defective within a specified period of time. One problem with guarantees and warranties is that they are often explained in complex, legal language that is hidden in small print. The car dealer probably gave you a booklet containing the warranty details. Unless you recorded the salesperson's oral promises at the point of sale, however, you are not likely to have any recourse. Always take your time and carefully read the details of warranties and guarantees.

Price Claims

Advertising shall avoid price claims which are false or misleading, or saving claims which do not offer provable savings.

You see a jewelry store ad claiming the store will be lowering the prices of its products by 70 percent on Saturday. So you decide to visit the store to buy a friend's birthday present. But once you arrive, you notice some problems. First, only select items are included in the 70 percent sale. None of the jewelry you are interested in buying is on sale. And when you look closely at the pieces that are included in the sale, you see that the presale prices are unrealistically high. A bracelet that you thought would sell for about $50 has an original price of $200. When the 70 percent discount is applied, the sale price drops to $60, about what you thought the price should have been in the first place. You leave the store empty-handed, feeling that the store has deceived you and wasted your time.

While fairness and honesty in price claims are required by the advertising code of ethics, violations of this principle are difficult to prove. Precisely what constitutes an unfairly high presale price? In addition, consumers are bombarded with a constant stream of sale ads, resulting in the fact that many people fail to notice the small print containing disclaimers.

Testimonials

Advertising containing testimonials shall be limited to those of competent witnesses who are reflecting a real and honest opinion or experience.

A **testimonial** is an endorsement of a product by someone claiming to have benefited from its use. Advertisements often feature celebrities and experts touting the wonders of various products. Over the years, this practice has proven to be a very effective sales technique. But there are some ethical limitations on how these testimonials are conducted. Read the examples below and see if you think they violate the spirit of this principle.

- "I'm not a doctor, but I play one on TV. Buy Brand A cough syrup."
- "I'm an actor, not a lawyer. But if you are injured in an accident, you should call 1-800-sue-someone."
- "I'm a mom, and I recommend Brand B bandages."
- "I used to be a television star. Now I'm recommending that you buy life insurance from Brand C."

Notice how vaguely this principle was written. What constitutes "competent witnesses"? Should they be required to have some measure of specific expertise? After all, anyone is capable of a "real and honest opinion or experience."

Taste and Decency

Advertising shall be free of statements, illustrations or implications which are offensive to good taste or public decency.

On the surface, it appears that producing offensive ads would risk alienating the very audience that a company is trying to reach. The real world, however, is more complex. For example, a company may be trying to reach an audience that reacts positively to material that offends others. Ads that are broadcast on cable music video or comedy channels sometimes include material that offends viewers of more conservative programming. And advertisers do carefully choose when and where to air their commercials.

But edgy ads can have a spillover effect and unintended consequences. Some special interest groups closely monitor the advertisements in publications and broadcasts aimed at children and minors (or those to whom children and minors might have access; for example, parents and adults). When the monitoring groups find material they deem offensive or inappropriate, they may try to embarrass the sponsors into retracting the ads and replacing them with more appropriate content.

As the principle makes clear, advertisers do have a social obligation to avoid producing ads that are in poor taste or offensive. But what constitutes "good taste" and "public decency"? How many people must be offended for an ad to be considered offensive? The United States is a complex society that has many sub-cultures. Pleasing everyone all of the time is impossible. But deeply offending a particular group and coming across to the public as uncaring or crude can have disastrous consequences for a company.

Limitations of the Advertising Code of Ethics

In addition to the use of ambiguous language, the code of ethics you have been exploring has another limitation. For any code to be effective, it must be enforceable and actually enforced. And the lack of enforcement of the advertising code represents a problem. Membership in trade groups such as the AAF is voluntary. Unlike professions such as law and medicine, no one has to be licensed to be able to make a living as an advertiser. The AAF has no authority to revoke someone's license to advertise for violating the code. Conformity to the principles of the code is voluntary, as well.

Checkpoint

1. In your own words, explain the meaning and relevance of each of the following parts of the advertising code of ethics.

a. truth _____

_____

b. substantiation _____

_____

c. comparisons _____

_____

d. bait advertising _____

_____

e. guarantees and warranties _____

_____

f. price claims _____

_____

g. testimonials _____

_____

h. taste and decency _____

_____

2. Explain the problem of enforcing the advertising code of ethics.

_____

_____

What do you think now?

Consider Sam's story at the beginning of the chapter. Which parts of the advertising code of ethics could provide Sam with guidance? Explain what the code of ethics would imply that he do and why.

_____

_____

_____

_____

_____

Personal Reflection

Briefly describe a time when you had to choose between honesty and money. In other words, you could have gotten more money by being dishonest. What did you do? Why? How do you feel about your decision now?

Summary

Ethical issues relevant to the advertising profession include false advertising, puffery, the practice of bait and switch, concerns about advertising to children, and the proper use of telemarketing tools.

Advertisers have a code of ethics that attempts to establish an ethical standard for the field. Provisions of the code involve truth in advertising, substantiation of claims, comparisons with competitors, bait advertising, honoring of guarantees and warranties, fair and honest price claims, proper use of testimonials, and issues of taste and decency.

Vocabulary Builder

Match the following terms to their definitions.

1. _____ An assurance attesting to the durability or quality of a service or product.
2. _____ A written promise to repair or replace a product if it breaks or becomes defective within a specified period of time.
3. _____ A written set of principles and rules intended to serve as a guideline for ethical behavior for individuals under the organization's authority.
4. _____ An endorsement of a product by someone claiming to have benefited from its use.
5. _____ The validation of advertising claims with objective data from independent research.
6. _____ The practice of advertising a product at a low price while intentionally stocking only a limited number in hopes of luring shoppers to buy more expensive items.
7. _____ The practice of attracting public attention to a product or business for the purpose of increasing sales.
8. _____ The practice of selling directly to individuals through unsolicited phone calls, e-mails, or faxes.
9. _____ The practice of making statements about products that the advertiser knows are not true.
10. _____ The term used to describe statements that are not outright lies, but merely exaggerations.

a. advertising
b. bait and switch
c. code of ethics
d. false advertising
e. guarantee
f. puffery
g. substantiation
h. telemarketing
i. testimonial
j. warranty

Reinforcement

1. Working with a small group of classmates, create a product advertisement that violates as many parts of the AAF's code of ethics as possible. Share your ad with or demonstrate your ad to the class.

_____

_____

_____

_____

2. Create another product advertisement that does not violate the code of ethics. Share this ad with or demonstrate this ad to the class, as well.

_____

_____

_____

_____

Thinking Critically

1. Use the ETHICS model to find the wisest possible solution to Deon's dilemma.

Deon is a new employee at a national advertising company. He is thrilled to have the job of his dreams so soon after graduating from college. His first assignment is to help create television ads for a national chain of steak house restaurants. But Deon is a vegetarian and fervently believes that eating meat is morally wrong. If he participates in this project, he will be encouraging people to do something that he is convinced they should not do. However, because this is his first project for the company, his superiors are watching him carefully. First impressions are important, and he desperately wants to make a good one.

evaluate the problem: _____

_____

_____

think through the options: _____

_____

_____

highlight the stakeholders: _____

_____

_____

identify and apply relevant ethical principles: _____

_____

_____

_____

_____

choose the wisest option: _____

_____

_____

state your justification: _____

_____

_____

2. What changes would you make to the advertising code of ethics to make it more effective in regulating the actions of advertisers?

_____

_____

_____

Digging Deeper

1. Have a class contest to see who can document the most examples of unethical advertising over a specific period of time. Bonus points will be given to the student who finds the single most unethical ad!

2. Interview a business owner or an advertising professional about his or her views on ethics in advertising. Create your own list of at least three questions to ask. Share your findings in an oral presentation to the class.

Personal Reflection

1. The most important ideas that I learned in this chapter were

2. This chapter made me think about

3. I would like to find out more about

4. One step I could take toward being a wiser consumer of advertising is

6 Ethics and Selling

After completing this chapter, you should be able to:

■ Explain key ethical problems and concerns relevant to the practice of selling.

■ Identify a variety of principles of honest and ethical selling.

Key Terms & Concepts

selling	commission	conflict of interest
price gouging	straight commission	fraud
false prizes	class-action lawsuit	

What do you think?

Terrence just started his first full-time job, working for a company that sells magazine subscriptions. He learns that, while the company utilizes many selling strategies, the most profitable department is telephone sales, where he will be working. But Terrence is already starting to feel uncomfortable. At the orientation for new employees, the corporate sales director describes the company's philosophy as "Sell! Sell! Sell!" "Don't do anything illegal," she adds, "but do whatever you must to make the sale." She also points out that the salespeople are paid a percentage of every subscription. "If you don't sell magazines," she warns, "you don't get paid."

Terrence's supervisor, Joel, tells him that the secret to success in telephone sales is to locate senior citizens living alone and sell them everything possible. "They love having someone to talk to on the phone," Joel said, "and they often forget which magazines, if any, they already subscribe to. You can talk them into almost anything. We've sometimes sold 30 or 40 subscriptions to the same person!"

Terrence wants to be successful in his new job, and he already knows that he can take home a decent paycheck. But he doesn't feel good about manipulating and exploiting anyone, especially vulnerable seniors. He can't help but think about his own grandmother and how he would feel if someone took advantage of her in this way.

Should he give the job a chance or listen to his conscience and take a stand? But then again, how will it look to other employers if he quits during the first week of his first job?

What do you think?

Each year The Gallup Organization surveys Americans on their perceptions of the honesty and ethics of people in different professions. Here are the results of one recent poll. The number beside each profession represents the percentage of people who ranked that profession's ethics as *high* or *very high.*

1. Nurses (82%)
2. Druggists/Pharmacists (67%)
3. Medical doctors (65%)
4. High school teachers (64%)
5. Law enforcement officers (61%)
6. Clergy (54%)
7. Funeral directors (44%)
8. Bankers (41%)
9. Accountants (39%)
10. Journalists (28%)
11. Real estate agents (20%)
12. Building contractors (20%)
13. Lawyers (18%)
14. Labor union leaders (16%)
15. Senators (16%)
16. Business executives (16%)
17. Stockbrokers (16%)
18. Congresspersons (14%)
19. Advertising practitioners (11%)
20. Car salesmen (8%)
21. Telemarketers (7%)

Source: Jeffrey M. Jones, "Nurses Remain Atop Honesty and Ethics List: Hold Substantial Lead Over Other Professions," Gallup News Service, December 05, 2005.

Notice that four of the bottom five professions are directly or indirectly related to selling. Why do you suppose that is? What is it about the practice of selling that leads people to discount the ethics of those who sell for a living? Can salespeople be honest and ethical and still make money?

You Decide

What makes a selling technique seem ethical or unethical to you? Beside each of the following selling scenarios, circle *ethical* or *unethical* and explain why you made that choice.

1. A salesperson at a gym is trying to convince a customer to purchase a long-term membership. The salesperson says, "I'm saying this as a friend; you need to join because you aren't going to attract anyone romantically looking the way you do."

   Ethical   Unethical   Why? _____

2. A salesperson tries to convince a customer to buy a car from her dealership by telling stories about how dishonest and unethical the dealership's main competitor is.

   Ethical   Unethical   Why? _____

3. A local building supply store triples the price of lumber after a storm damages many homes in the area.

   Ethical   Unethical   Why? _____

4. A telemarketer begins sales calls by stating, "Please stay on the line; this isn't a sales call."

   Ethical   Unethical   Why? _____

5. A housing developer entices potential customers to tour his homes by telling people they are guaranteed to win one of the following prizes: (1) a new car, (2) $10,000, or (3) a refrigerator. In truth, everyone who takes the tour (and sits through a two-hour sales pitch) "wins" a tiny battery-operated plastic cooler that holds three beverage cans.

   Ethical   Unethical   Why? _____

"The reward of a thing well done is to have done it."

—Ralph Waldo Emerson

Personal Reflection

Write about a time when you were cheated or exploited by someone who sold you something. How did you feel about the experience then? How do you feel about the experience now?

Ethical Problems and Concerns in Selling

Selling is the practice of exchanging goods for money. People often participate in the processes of buying and selling. One person with an item of some value wants to exchange it for money. Another person with money wants to exchange it for the item of value. A mutually acceptable arrangement is made, and the sale is made.

Selling is a simple process. However, when a person's income is based on his or her ability to sell products, the situation gets more complex. When a person's only goal is to make a sale, that person may begin to think that the end justifies the means—that anything that helps him or her make the sale is permissible. Many salespeople are honorable, honest individuals. But the actions of a small number of dishonest, exploitive salespeople have created the negative perceptions demonstrated in the Gallup Poll numbers. Moreover, the tremendous pressure to succeed can sometimes lead even good people to make poor ethical decisions. This section will explore some of the dishonest sales practices that can result, as well as look for a deeper cause of those practices.

Lying and Manipulation

Why did the Gallup survey list the specific job of car salesman? Why not refrigerator or cosmetics salespeople? After all, there are honest and dishonest people in every corner of the business world. Why single out the people who sell cars?

You probably already know the answer to that question. The stereotype of people who sell automobiles is one of dishonesty and manipulation—that they do and say anything to get customers to buy their cars. As with all stereotypes, the one about car salespeople does not fit everyone who sells cars for a living. People of integrity and honor sell cars while treating their customers with honesty and fairness. But the stereotype continues, apparently because a sufficient number of car salespeople cheat their customers.

In addition to being unethical and illegal, lying to and manipulating customers are self-defeating behaviors. In the short term, the practices may result in more money for the salesperson, but then what? How many customers will return to a dealership that they believe cheated them previously?

Price Gouging

Price gouging is the practice of pricing a product far above the normal market value on the basis that consumers have no other way to buy the product. Some lumber stores have drastically raised the price of home repair products after destructive storms. When electricity goes out, bags of ice may sell for $20; electric generators may triple in price overnight. Supply and demand can sometimes run amuck.

Price gouging is illegal in most states and, fortunately, seems to be occurring with less frequency. Law enforcement officials and the news media monitor stores carefully after disasters, watching for any signs that unscrupulous businesses might try to profit unfairly from the suffering of others.

False Prizes

A fairly common sales technique that tricks potential customers into thinking they have won valuable prizes such as cash, cars, and cruises is the practice of offering **false prizes**. Sometimes victims are told that they must pay service or delivery charges before they can collect the prize. In truth, the prize doesn't exist and the money disappears. Another technique is to use the lure of a prize to get customers to listen to a sales pitch about a different product. In those cases, the prize (usually a disappointment) is awarded after the sales talk.

It is illegal for a business to promise a customer something and then break that promise. But those who utilize the false prize technique have found creative loopholes in the consumer laws. The loopholes are often explained in very small print. The "free cruise" may not include a variety of charges, taxes, and tips that add up to the price of a regular ticket. The "free vacation" may be a few days in a low-quality motel that you would never stay in otherwise. The "free piano" may turn out to be a toy keyboard.

A good rule of thumb in life is that if something sounds too good to be true, it usually is. But many people become excited at the thought of winning a prize, and unethical people count on that.

Commission

Why do some salespeople resort to unethical sales techniques? The short answer is because of money. But it goes deeper than that. Teachers are paid money for what they do, but can you imagine a teacher lying to students to get an extra homework assignment out of them? Would a school bus driver deceive parents to get more children to ride the bus? Would a police officer alter a speed limit sign so he or she could hand out more citations? What's the difference in sales?

Many businesses pay their sales staff on **commission**. This means that the company rewards salespeople with a percentage of the money they make from sales. The more the employees sell, the more they earn. Some companies go a step further and pay their sales staff on **straight commission**. This means that the employees get no salary or hourly wage; their income is based entirely on what they sell.

Being paid on commission motivates people to work hard to sell products. Many companies believe that paying their salespeople this way produces more sales and higher revenue for the business. On the other hand, the practice also can encourage deceptive and dishonest sales techniques.

Many argue that paying employees on commission is one of the problems behind other ethical problems in sales. Human greed lurks in the background, and the practice of paying commission sometimes gives the greatest rewards to the least ethical people. But ethical people can be affected, too. If the end of the month is near and an employee has not yet made enough money to pay his or her bills, the temptation to bend ethical and legal rules may become very strong.

Several years ago the automotive repair department of a national chain of retail stores lost a **class-action lawsuit**, a suit brought on behalf of a large group of people. In this case, the group consisted of customers who believed they had been cheated by the company. During the course of the trial, evidence was presented that the company paid its mechanics on commission. The more the mechanics charged in repairs, the higher their commissions. Some mechanics were even alleged to have damaged cars intentionally so they could repair them and make more money!

> "We make a living by what we get, but we make a life by what we give."
> —Winston Churchill

Conflict of Interest

The practice of paying salespeople on commission has another consequence, too. It creates a potential conflict of interest for the sales staff. A **conflict of interest** occurs when people's professional decisions and actions are influenced by their personal interests. When an individual takes his or her car to an automotive shop, the mechanic's job is to meet the customer's needs, that is, to serve the car's owner by accurately diagnosing and repairing the problem. But if the mechanic's personal interests are furthered by making the customer pay more money, then it is not difficult to see the potential conflict.

The result is a loss of trust. Are you more likely to trust the advice of a salesperson who gets to keep a percentage of what he or she convinces you to spend or the advice of a salesperson who gets paid the same amount whether or not you make a purchase? Even when commissioned salespeople are honest, customers still may not trust their advice. And more than anything else, that lack of trust is why car salesmen and telemarketers ranked at the very bottom of the Gallup Poll survey.

Fortunately, more companies are beginning to understand the connection between gaining customer trust and paying on commission. One outcome of the lawsuit mentioned previously was that the company being sued had to agree to stop the practice of paying its mechanics on commission. Moreover, some retail stores now advertise that their sales associates are not paid on commission. The message to consumers is clear: Our employees are here to help you, not just to sell our products.

Checkpoint

In your own words, explain each of the following concepts, issues, or concerns.

selling _____
_____

lying and manipulation _____
_____

price gouging _____
_____

false prizes _____
_____

commission _____
_____

straight commission _____
_____

class-action lawsuit _____
_____

conflict of interest _____
_____

What do you think now?

Review the scenario that involved Terrence at the beginning of the chapter. List three ethical issues or concerns that you see in the story. Write a sentence for each issue or concern, explaining why it represents an actual or potential ethical problem.

_____
_____
_____
_____
_____

Write about a time when you, or someone you know, sold or tried to sell something and were less than honest or fair with the buyer. If given the opportunity to relive that experience, what could be done differently?

Real-World Ethics

What causes people to act unethically in the workplace? According to a recent survey by the American Management Association, the answer might surprise you. The researchers found that the most common cause of employee misdeeds is not greed, a desire to further one's career, or even an attempt to protect one's job. Instead, almost 70 percent of those surveyed blamed their ethical misdeeds on the pressure imposed by supervisors and administrators to meet unrealistic goals and deadlines. Corporate executives, under great pressure to succeed, often pass that pressure down the ladder to rank-and-file employees. Trying to further one's career came in a distant second.

©Getty Images/PhotoDisc

"It is easier to fight for principles than to live up to them."

—Alfred Adler

Consumers may be so used to others trying to deceive and manipulate them into buying things that they have become numb to the practice. At some point, they may have assumed that those kinds of tactics are the only way that salespeople can effectively sell products. Assuming for a moment that ethical selling is possible, what would it look like?

Principles of Ethical Selling

The good news is that selling does not have to be manipulative, deceptive, or disrespectful to be effective. Most people in most professions are honest and honorable people. Many people make excellent incomes in sales while treating their customers with integrity and fairness. So how do salespeople think and act differently to sell products honestly and ethically?

Think Long-Term

The majority of unethical business actions and decisions are based on short-term thinking. People sometimes think in terms of acquiring money immediately, which can lead to cutting corners and taking shortcuts. But people are not generally thinking about the long-term consequences of their actions. They may make more money at the moment, but they will have repercussions to deal with as a result of their actions.

A merchant can fool customers into buying a poorly made, defective, or overpriced product. But what happens after the sale? The cheated customers are not likely to buy from that store in the future, and they are very likely to tell their friends and family about the negative experience. Honest, ethical selling requires mature, long-term thinking. It makes far more sense (and results in higher profits) for a merchant to satisfy the customer, resulting in repeat business for many years, than to cheat the customer even once, resulting in lost sales.

Elevate the Goal

The goal of a sales call is no longer limited to selling a product to a customer, but to create a mutually beneficial relationship. This new focus changes everything about the conversations between salespeople and customers. There is no reason for manipulation or lying. People are not viewed as wallets to be exploited, but relationships to be built and nurtured.

Recall Immanuel Kant's principle of *respect for persons*. Kant said that it is always wrong to exploit other people—to use them in ways that harm them for one's personal benefit or gain. One of the reasons salespeople ranked so low on the survey of professional ethics is that the traditional model of selling has been closely linked with manipulation and exploitation (and no one likes being manipulated or exploited). Ethical selling means acting for the customers' best interests, not merely trying to get customers' money.

"The effects of our actions may be postponed, but they are never lost."

—Chinese proverb

Change the Tactics

Never lie to, deceive, or manipulate potential customers. Lying doesn't work in the long term or in the short term. Many consumers today are experienced, savvy shoppers. They have been deceived by exploitive salespeople enough times to know that they must be on guard, expecting the deceptive tactics.

For a company, the result of its dishonesty and deception may be not only lost sales, but also much more. A customer who can prove that a salesperson was deceptive is a potential lawsuit for a company. The legal expenses and lost judgments can be very expensive for a business and may lead to bankruptcy. Employers cannot afford to keep employees who may get the company sued.

Learn to Listen

The traditional model of selling involves memorizing the key points of a sales talk, presenting that information to consumers, and hoping the sales pitch will convince some listeners to buy. Questions asked of consumers are often designed to lead them to a decision to buy. Unsolicited questions from consumers are considered distractions. The process of selling is canned and planned.

Put yourself in the customers' shoes. Does that sound like the kind of conversation you want to have when you go shopping? Do you want to listen to someone talk about a product, or would you rather have someone listen to what you need? Which approach would be more likely to win your business?

Forget the sales pitch; listen to the customer.

Ethics & Law

Lying and deceiving customers can sometimes reach the point where it constitutes legal **fraud**, deliberately deceiving people to secure unlawful or unfair gain. Fraud convictions often result in prison terms and huge fines, sometimes even bankruptcy. Wise companies think long-term and realize that in the long run, they are better off being honest and fair.

Checkpoint

In your own words, summarize each of the aspects of honest, ethical selling.

think long-term _____

_____

elevate the goal _____

_____

change the tactics _____

_____

learn to listen _____

_____

What do you think now?

Reconsider Terrence's story at the beginning of the chapter. What would need to be different for Terrence's employer to be an ethical company? Revise the story, changing all of the unethical issues and concerns that you identified earlier into honest and ethical selling practices.

_____

_____

_____

_____

_____

_____

Personal Reflection

What do you think about the concept of ethical selling? In your opinion, can a salesperson be successful in the long term, maybe even more successful, by utilizing ethical practices? Explain your answer.

Learn More

Use the Internet to research the Direct Selling Association's Code of Ethics. What selling practices are prohibited by the code? What standards are required? How are the rules and principles enforced?

Summary

Several ethical issues and concerns are relevant to the profession of selling. They include lying and manipulation, price gouging, false prizes, commissions, and conflict of interest. These types of actions often stem from short-term thinking and the pressure to make immediate sales by any means necessary.

Ethical selling includes thinking long-term, building relationships with customers, dedicating oneself to honesty, and listening carefully to the needs and concerns of potential buyers. Selling products with honesty and integrity is more likely to lead to increased customer loyalty and repeat buyers.

Vocabulary Builder

Match the following terms to their definitions.

1. _____ Deliberately deceiving people to secure unlawful or unfair gain.
2. _____ Employees get no salary or hourly wage; their income is based entirely on what they sell.
3. _____ Occurs when people's professional decisions and actions are influenced by their personal interests.
4. _____ The practice of exchanging goods for money.
5. _____ The practice of pricing a product far above the normal market value on the basis that consumers have no other way to buy the product.
6. _____ Rewarding salespeople with a percentage of the money from the sales they make.
7. _____ A suit brought on behalf of a large group of people.

a. class-action lawsuit
b. commission
c. conflict of interest
d. fraud
e. price gouging
f. selling
g. straight commission

Reinforcement

1. Create a sales pitch for a product, including as many unethical tactics as you can. Make your pitch to a classmate. Have your partner share how the tactics would have made him or her feel as a potential customer. Then switch roles, letting your partner make the sales pitch to you. Afterward discuss how you would have felt as the customer.

_____

_____

_____

_____

2. Repeat the exercise above, but this time follow the guidelines of ethical selling.

_____

_____

_____

_____

Thinking Critically

1. Use the ETHICS model to find the wisest possible solution to Meredith's dilemma below.

Meredith is a salesperson for a retail electronics store. She is also a single mother of three children, ranging in age from five to twelve. Because Meredith is paid a small hourly wage, she needs the commission from her sales to support her family. Being an ethical person is very important to Meredith. She understands that her self-respect depends on that, and she wants to be a positive role model for her children.

One problem Meredith has with her job is that it appears that the salespeople who receive the biggest paychecks are the ones using deceptive, manipulative sales techniques. They also are often the first to be considered for promotions. Meredith is discouraged. She knows that she would sell more products if she used these underhanded tactics, and she is tempted to do so. She really needs the extra income to provide for her children. But how can she teach them to be honest if she isn't?

evaluate the problem: _____

_____

think through the options: _____

_____

highlight the stakeholders: _____

_____

identify and apply relevant ethical principles: _____

_____

_____

_____

choose the wisest option: _____

_____

state your justification: _____

_____

_____

2. Provide one additional principle as part of an ethical approach to selling. Explain your principle.

_____

_____

_____

Digging Deeper

1. Interview someone who makes a living in sales. Ask for the person's opinions about the unethical sales practices discussed in this chapter. What does he or she think about the concept of ethical selling? Summarize your findings in an e-mail to your instructor or in a short paragraph to hand in.

2. Use the Internet to find examples of (a) unethical sales tactics or (b) ethical selling practices. Choose one web site to share with the class.

3. Conduct a survey of students and teachers at your school, or friends and relatives. Ask them (1) what unethical sales techniques irritate them the most and (2) what aspects of positive sales experiences they appreciate the most. Summarize your results and present your findings to the class.

Personal Reflection

1. The most important ideas that I learned in this chapter were

2. This chapter made me think about

3. I would like to find out more about

4. One step that I could take to better protect myself against unethical sales practices is

7

Ethics and Finance

After completing this chapter, you should be able to:

■ Identify and explain common ethical issues relevant to finance.

■ Apply universal ethical principles to those issues to make sound moral judgments.

Key Terms & Concepts

finance	credit report	churning
audit	fiduciary obligation	insider trading
usury		

Farah started her freshman year at State University. She spent the first week moving into her dorm room, buying books, finding classrooms, and getting settled into her new life. One aspect of college life that surprised her was the many credit card applications she received. Farah would often find three or four new credit card ads in her mailbox. Credit card companies had set up tables all around campus, offering T-shirts, dorm supplies, and other gifts to students who submitted applications.

Farah asked one of her professors about what she was experiencing. The instructor told her that college students are frequently targeted by credit card companies. "You're adults now and legally responsible for your financial decisions. But many students don't have much spending money and often don't understand how credit cards work. They think it's free money. By the time they figure out the truth, they may be thousands of dollars in debt, and their credit is ruined for years. In fact, some college students graduate owing more on their credit cards than on their student loans!"

Farah is tempted by the offers. Many of the advertisements claim to charge 0 percent interest. She hasn't read all of the small print, but those claims sound like free money to her. Besides, she's sure she will find a great job when she graduates. She can pay off the credit cards then.

What do you think?

Read these short scenarios. Rate each one according to how serious an ethical concern you think the scenario represents. Circle the number on the scale. After each rating, write one sentence explaining why you rated the scenario as you did.

A. A bank has an unwritten policy of rejecting mortgage applications from an economically disadvantaged neighborhood populated mostly by members of a racial minority group.

1	2	3	4	5
No ethical concern	Minor ethical concern	Moderate ethical concern	Important ethical concern	Very serious ethical concern

Explanation: _____

B. Concerned that their corporation may be in financial trouble, top executives quietly sell off their company stock while assuring employees and investors that the company is in great shape and expecting high profits.

1	2	3	4	5
No ethical concern	Minor ethical concern	Moderate ethical concern	Important ethical concern	Very serious ethical concern

Explanation: _____

"Money often costs too much."
—Ralph Waldo Emerson

C. A corporation pays bonuses to its accounting staff based on how low the company's tax debt is at the end of each year.

1	2	3	4	5
No ethical concern	Minor ethical concern	Moderate ethical concern	Important ethical concern	Very serious ethical concern

Explanation: _____

D. A credit card company advertises an initial interest rate of 0 percent. In small print on the back of the ad are the facts that the rate jumps to 13.99 percent after six months and to 24.99 percent if the consumer ever makes a late payment. The company reserves the right to change the terms at any time.

1	2	3	4	5
No ethical concern	Minor ethical concern	Moderate ethical concern	Important ethical concern	Very serious ethical concern

Explanation: _____

E. An investment company pays its "investment consultants" a commission on every stock that clients buy or sell, subtly encouraging the employees to persuade clients to make trades, even when it might not be in the clients' best interests.

1	2	3	4	5
No ethical concern	Minor ethical concern	Moderate ethical concern	Important ethical concern	Very serious ethical concern

Explanation: _____

Personal Reflection

Write down one wise thing you have done with money at some point in your life. Also write down one unwise financial decision you have made. What motivated you to make each decision?

Wise:

    Motivation:

Unwise:

    Motivation:

You are sitting in a chair across from a person of "infinite" wealth who is handing you a $20 bill every 30 seconds, one after another after another. The person tells you that she will stop giving you the bills whenever you tell her that you have all you want and do not want any more. How much money would be enough to satisfy you? ten thousand dollars? a million dollars? Some people might sit in that chair a long, long time, never able to enjoy what the money might buy because they cannot bring themselves to say "That's enough." Would you be one of those people?

Take out a dollar bill and look at it closely. (If you don't have a single, a $5, $10, or $20 bill will work just as well.) Have you ever considered what gives money its value? After all, you are holding little more than a finely detailed piece of paper. In and of itself, the bill is worth no more than a scrap of old newspaper. But the fact that its value is guaranteed by the United States Department of the Treasury is important. To some people, those finely detailed pieces of paper hold a lot of meaning.

It has been said that money makes the world go around. Laws of physics aside, that does seem true at times. So many daily decisions made by individuals, families, businesses, and governments are based on obtaining money. It is true that some of the decisions have negative results, but that doesn't mean that money is a bad thing. In modern societies, money is necessary to buy food, shelter, clothing, and other goods that people need and want. But because money seems to have the power to cause both good and bad in people's lives, wherever money is, ethical issues seem to be swirling about.

"Happiness is not in the mere possession of money; it lies in the joy of achievement, in the thrill of creative effort."

—Franklin D. Roosevelt

Ethical Issues in Financial Professions

Finance is the management of money, banking, investments, and other assets. People in the field of finance work in a wide variety of professions, including banking, investment advising, loan management, accounting, and management of corporate financial assets. Those jobs can help people improve the quality of their lives and can help companies to prosper and flourish. However, unethical and illegal actions on the part of financial professionals may result in serious harm to individuals, communities, and businesses.

Accounting

Imagine a situation in which an accounting firm is conducting an extensive financial audit of a major corporation. An **audit** is an examination of financial records or accounts to check their accuracy. Stockholders and potential investors are waiting impatiently for the results of the examination, as the company's stock value may rise or fall depending on the final report. As the release of the report nears, a journalist writes a story pointing out that one branch of the accounting firm offers financial management consulting services to corporations. As it turns out, the consulting department's biggest client is the same company that the firm is currently auditing. The reporter equates the practice to a basketball coach refereeing a game played by his or her own team.

Honesty and accuracy are core professional duties of accountants, and both depend on the accountant's ability to remain objective and unbiased. The kind of dual relationship between accounting firms and corporations described earlier brings objectivity, integrity, and bias into question. Acting simultaneously as accountant and financial consultant would appear to be an obvious *conflict of interest,* a situation in which people's professional decisions and actions are influenced by their personal interests. Surprisingly, until recently, the practice was legal. But after a series of corporate ethics scandals and bankruptcies, the U.S. Congress passed the *Sarbanes-Oxley Act.* While the legislation is immensely complex and broad in scope, one clear intention is to prohibit dual relationships between accounting firms and corporations.

 ## Real-World Ethics

©Digital Vision

What motivates corporate executives to run their companies ethically? A recent study by the Human Resource Institute found that the most common reason given by business leaders is to protect the company's reputation. It is far more cost-efficient for companies to maintain the trust of the public, customers, and investors than to try to win that trust back after it has been damaged. The second reason given by executives was that being ethical is simply the right thing to do. In the words of an old French proverb, "There is no pillow as soft as a clear conscience."

Banking and Lending

Some people still think of banks primarily in terms of savings and checking accounts. Customers put their money in the bank, collect a little interest on it, and take the money out when they need it. But the world has experienced a revolution over the past few decades. Contemporary banking is more about loans and credit cards.

The ability to borrow money allows people to purchase goods that are difficult, perhaps even impossible, to save for. How long would it take to save $25,000 for a car or $250,000 for a house? Car loans and home mortgages allow people to enjoy their purchases now and pay for them over time. Consumer purchases lead to prosperous businesses, higher employment, a healthy stock market, and a strong economy.

However, important ethical issues are at stake. Many people have learned the hard way that it is much easier to borrow money than to pay it back. Interest rates, finance charges, and temptingly low minimum payments can keep people trapped in debt for many years. Meanwhile, new expenses often arise. The car needs repairs, the refrigerator breaks, the family needs a vacation. More money is borrowed. At some point, the borrower finds that he or she is barely able to make the minimum payments each month. On top of that, the person may get sick or lose his or her job.

The pressure to maximize profits can lead lenders to some ethically questionable behaviors. Some banks and credit card companies have been criticized for encouraging people to borrow more money than they can afford to pay back and for practicing **usury**, charging excessively high interest rates. In ancient times, *usury* meant charging *any* interest on loaned money; in the sacred writings of some major world religions, it was actually prohibited. Today, with approximately nine thousand credit cards competing for customers, advertising a high interest rate puts a company at a disadvantage. Therefore, companies tend to advertise very low rates that rise dramatically after an introductory period—perhaps six months. In addition, annual fees, finance charges, and exorbitant late fees can work in tandem with high interest rates to keep people locked into debt.

Lenders defend their policies by pointing out that the terms and conditions of their loans are spelled out in print on their loan applications. In addition, when deciding whether to loan individuals money and how much to loan them, lenders rely heavily on credit reports.

A **credit report** is a history and summary of a person's personal credit history. It includes information on where the person lives and whether he or she has been arrested or sued. It shows how the person pays his or her bills and whether he or she has filed for bankruptcy. That information is collected by three nationwide consumer reporting companies—TransUnion, Experian, and Equifax. Those companies make money by selling credit reports to lenders, employers, insurers, and other businesses. The information is used in evaluating credit and insurance applications, making employment decisions, and renting homes. It's not difficult to see why having a good credit score is important!

The federal Fair Credit Reporting Act requires each of the consumer reporting companies to provide individuals who make a request with one free copy of their credit report each year. You may have seen advertisements by companies that will obtain the reports for a fee, but there is no reason to pay for the service. The Federal Trade Commission (FTC) maintains a web site instructing people on how to access their free credit reports.

> "Never work just for money or for power. They won't save your soul or help you sleep at night."
>
> —Marian Wright Edelman

Investment and Financial Advising

Many people try to make money through investing—purchasing shares of stock in businesses, buying government bonds, trading in commodities, or investing in mutual funds that combine some or all of those options. Those people are hoping that whatever they invest in will increase in value over time.

If that happens, they make a profit. But, of course, investments do not always work out as people hope. Sometimes the value of the investment stays about the same. Or sometimes the value goes down, and people lose some or all of their investment.

Financial professionals are involved in investing. After all, an individual cannot simply walk up to the cash register at a gas station and buy shares of stock in the oil company that owns the station. Investment companies, stockbrokers, and financial advisors serve as bridges between investors and investments. Once under contract, these financial professionals are required to act in the investors' interests. This responsibility to act in a client's interests instead of one's own is called a **fiduciary obligation**. When that duty is violated, legal and ethical rules are broken.

One such violation is referred to as churning. An investor depends on the broker's financial expertise and knowledge of the markets. However, brokerage companies often make a commission from each investment bought or sold. **Churning** is the practice of encouraging investors to make multiple unnecessary trades in order to create extra income for the broker.

Another important legal and ethical issue is insider trading. Knowledge is the most important ingredient in investing. The more a person knows about a company, the better he or she can predict the future value of its stock. But the executives who manage a company have the most knowledge about the financial details of their firm. What if corporate leaders, knowing the company is in trouble, decide to sell their own shares of stock before anyone else finds out? Would that seem fair to you if you were one of the new investors who bought stock in the firm?

Insider trading is the practice of buying or selling shares of stock or other investments on the basis of information that is not available to the public. Insider trading is illegal. The U.S. Securities and Exchange Commission (SEC) is charged with monitoring investments to prevent insider trading and other unfair investment practices.

Checkpoint

In your own words, write the meaning of each term.

finance _____

_____

audit _____

_____

usury _____

_____

credit report _____

_____

churning _____

_____

fiduciary obligation _____

_____

insider trading _____

_____

What do you think now?

Consider Farah's scenario at the beginning of the chapter. Whose fault do you think it is when people end up so far in debt that they have a difficult time seeing their way clear? Do you tend to blame the individuals for being financially irresponsible or the credit card companies for going to great lengths to encourage people to borrow more and more money? Explain your answer and be ready to discuss the issue in class.

_____

_____

_____

_____

_____

_____

Personal Reflection

Which ethical issue in the financial professions do you think has the greatest potential to cause people harm? Why?

Applying Ethical Principles to Financial Issues

As you have learned, legal standards and ethical standards are not always the same. Ethical actions may be illegal, as Martin Luther King, Jr., pointed out in his famous "Letter from the Birmingham Jail." (See Real-World Ethics in Chapter 1.) And just because an action is legal doesn't mean it's ethically or morally right. The ethical standard is based on universal ethical principles—the kind you read about in Chapter 2. This section will take a fresh look at those principles to see how they apply to ethical issues in finance.

The Egoism Principle

The *egoism principle* is the idea that the right thing for a person to do in any situation is the action that best serves that person's long-term interests. At first glance, this principle might seem to justify some unethical actions on the part of financial professionals. But remember, the key is *long-term*.

What are the long-term consequences of insider trading? Someone might get away with it a few times, but too many people are watching for insider trading to continue very long. Complex computer systems monitor stock trades and alert authorities to questionable transactions. Individuals convicted of insider trading can receive heavy fines, prison time, and the loss of lucrative jobs and careers.

The same rule of thumb applies to companies. Smart business leaders and policy makers think long-term. The abuse of dual relationships between accounting firms and major corporations resulted in a loss of public trust in accounting and led the federal government to pass new, very restrictive accounting laws.

Similarly, banks that consistently lure customers into excessive and unmanageable debt may eventually face an angry backlash from the public. Another result may be new laws that protect consumers from exploitive lenders.

> "Capital as such is not evil; it is its wrong use that is evil. Capital in some form or other will always be needed."
>
> —Gandhi

The Utility Principle

The *utility principle* is the idea that the morally right action is the one that produces the greatest possible good for the greatest number of people. Since there are more customers and consumers than businesses that serve them, this would seem, on the surface, to mean that whatever is best for consumers must be right. Perhaps banks should not charge interest for loans, but, instead, should offer high interest rates for savings accounts. Maybe investment companies should assume all risk for stock losses and let investors keep their gains. What a wonderful world it could be!

The reason those ideas won't work may sound familiar—because of the long-term implications. What would happen in the long term if banks and investment companies gave out more money than they took in? They would go out of business. Consumers would then be worse off without those important services. What is actually the greatest good for the greatest number is to allow financial companies to earn sustainable profits, but to diligently protect consumers from exploitation.

The Principle of Rights

According to the *principle of rights*, an action is considered moral when it respects the rights of others and is considered immoral when it violates another's rights. On the surface, the application of this principle seems simple. Financial service companies should respect the rights of their customers. But this is one of those situations where *legal* and *ethical* are not quite the same.

Laws allow people to forfeit or sign away their basic rights. If Ereka takes Manny's money by force, Manny's rights are violated. But what if Manny voluntarily signs a contract stating that Ereka may take his money? That fact changes everything.

You can compare that situation to the argument made by credit card companies and other lenders: "If people have other borrowing options and still choose to borrow money from us and if our terms are clearly stated in the contract, then how can we be exploiting people?" But individuals with poor credit histories may not have other borrowing options. Since they represent higher risks for lenders, many banks and credit card companies will not loan money to them. The ones that do offer loans are likely to charge higher interest rates.

In addition, what does "our terms are clearly stated in the contract" mean? Several pages of confusing legal terminology in small print might not meet the ethical standard, but it is all that the law requires. In the real world, consumers must protect themselves from individuals and companies that can violate their rights.

The Principle of Duties

The *principle of duties* maintains that you should do what is ethically right purely because you have a moral obligation to do what is ethically right. Do the right thing, not because good consequences will result, but because it's the right thing to do. The important point is that the duty is not to one's company, one's customers, or even one's community. The duty is simply to do the right thing.

How can people know their moral duties—the right things to do? Philosopher Immanuel Kant maintained that people's duties boil down to two basic concepts—universality and respect for persons. *Universality* is the idea that you should act as you would want others to act in the same situation. *Respect for persons* is the idea that it is always wrong to take unfair advantage of others for personal gain.

Applying those concepts to ethical issues in finance is not difficult, at least in principle. No rational person would want deception to be a universal moral standard because that would mean allowing oneself to be deceived. The same is true for conflicts of interest, usury, and other actions that can harm people financially. Since a person can't logically want others to harm him or her, it can't be right for that person to harm others. And the concept of respect for persons prohibits tactics that exploit others for personal gain, such as churning and manipulating people into borrowing more money than they can afford to repay.

However, those concepts are more difficult to live by in the real world. Pressure from stockholders to increase profits and dividends, combined with pressure from employees for increased wages and benefits, can lead company policy makers to seek profit-raising shortcuts. The short-term pressures work to make it more difficult for executives to keep their eyes on the long-term picture.

The Principle of Virtues

The *principle of virtues* is the idea that ethics is based on being a good person, that is, on incorporating ideal character traits, or virtues, into one's life. Proponents of this virtue tend to sum up the goal of ethics as *being good*. That viewpoint is currently very popular in business. Corporate leaders identify key virtues that they want their company to exhibit, such as integrity, fairness, truthfulness, respect, and generosity. Then the leaders work with employees and other stakeholder groups to determine the most effective ways to incorporate the virtues into company policies and practices. A common theme in current business ethics discussions is that *good ethics is good business.*

A strength of that approach is that people generally agree on the worthiness of the virtues. Not many people will argue that fairness and honesty are bad character traits. A potential weakness is the difficulty of translating the ideal traits into specific actions. For example, the interest rate on a loan doubles in six months. That fact is spelled out in small print on the credit application in the middle of several paragraphs of legal text. Is that arrangement sufficient for the company to praise itself for being honest and fair?

An important point to remember is that ethics is about being a good person, a good employee, a good citizen, and a good company. But ethics is also about doing the right thing and making the right decision when the pressure to do the wrong thing is strong. Wise business leaders who think long-term and want their companies to earn reputations for integrity and fairness try to incorporate as many universal ethical principles as possible into their decision-making processes.

Ethics & Law

The general purpose of laws is to reinforce social ethical standards. Societies that value honesty and fairness have laws designed to impose those standards on businesses. But people eventually stop conforming to laws that are not enforced. Therefore, federal, state, and local governments are charged with the responsibility of ensuring that people in businesses and professions obey the laws.

At the federal level, the FTC regulates general business practices. The SEC regulates investment-related trade, such as the stock market. The Federal Communications Commission (FCC) regulates issues related to broadcasting and telecommunications.

Checkpoint

In your own words, explain how each of the following ethical principles is relevant to people working in financial professions.

egoism principle _____

_____

_____

utility principle _____

_____

_____

principle of rights _____

_____

_____

principle of duties _____

_____

_____

principle of virtues _____

_____

_____

What do you think now?

Which ethical principles do you think the credit card companies in Farah's scenario were violating? Which principles, if any, do you think they were following? Be ready to explain and defend your opinions in a class discussion.

_____

_____

_____

_____

_____

_____

_____

_____

Personal Reflection

Which of the ethical principles discussed do you find yourself relying on most often when you are making ethical decisions? Which do you rely on the least? Why do you suppose that is?

Most

Why?

Least?

Why?

Learn More

Federal government regulatory agencies have their own web sites that describe their functions and provide resources for businesses and consumers. Use the Internet to explore the web sites of the FTC, SEC, and FCC. Find at least one useful fact about each organization to share with the class.

Summary

Ethical issues in professions related to finance include conflict of interest in accounting, usury and exploitation in lending, and churning and insider trading in investing. All of these ethical misdeeds can have serious economic consequences for customers and serious legal consequences for financial professionals.

The universal ethical principles of egoism, utility, rights, duties, and virtues can be applied to ethical issues in finance to help people in those professions make wise decisions. As with other business ethics issues, combining principles like these with long-term thinking can help prevent unethical actions.

Vocabulary Builder

Match the following terms to their definitions.

1. _____ Charging excessively high interest rates
2. _____ An examination of financial records or accounts to check their accuracy
3. _____ A history and summary of a person's personal credit history
4. _____ The illegal practice of buying or selling shares of stock or other investments on the basis of information that is not available to the public
5. _____ The management of money, banking, investments, and other assets
6. _____ The practice of encouraging investors to make multiple unnecessary trades in order to create extra income for the broker
7. _____ A professional responsibility to act in a client's interests instead of one's own

a. audit
b. churning
c. credit report
d. fiduciary obligation
e. finance
f. insider trading
g. usury

Reinforcement

1. You work for a credit card company. Create a new card with policies that are as unfair, deceptive, and exploitive as possible. Then create an advertisement whose goal is to induce customers into applying for your card.

_____

_____

_____

_____

_____

_____

_____

2. Create a new credit card with policies that are as honest and fair to consumers as possible, but that still remains profitable for your company. Create an advertisement for this card, too.

_____

_____

_____

_____

_____

_____

_____

Thinking Critically

1. Apply the ETHICS model to find the wisest, most ethical solution to Pete's dilemma.

Pete participates in an internship program conducted by his high school. He gains valuable experience in the workplace while earning high school credits at the same time. This semester Pete has been assigned to intern in the business offices of the Daisy-Fresh Carpet Cleaning Company. It is a small business owned by an older couple. Pete has been interning for only a few weeks, but overall he is pleased with the experience. He is already thinking about starting his own small business someday.

However, Pete has encountered one troubling issue. He has been learning basic bookkeeping and accounting and, therefore, has started helping the owners keep up with weekly expenses and income. Pete has noticed that the owners, Mr. and Mrs. Zarle, often change the numbers on invoices and receipts to make it look as though they make less money than they really do. He also has heard them offer discounts to customers who pay in cash and then observed that those cash transactions are not recorded properly, if at all, in the financial ledgers. The goal behind the accounting misdeeds is apparently to lower the income taxes that the Zarles will owe at the end of the year.

Pete has mixed feelings. He likes the owners, and they are treating him well. But it's clear that what they are doing is dishonest. Pete wants to talk to the Zarles about the issue, but he is afraid of angering and alienating them. Pete would like to get a positive referral from the couple when his internship ends, so upsetting them is not in his best interest. On the other hand, they seem like a nice couple who treat their customers fairly. Their company logo has the words *honesty* and *integrity* emblazoned on it. Pete doesn't understand how they can be so blatantly dishonest in this one area.

evaluate the problem: _____

_____

_____

think through the options: _____

_____

_____

_____

highlight the stakeholders: _____

_____

_____

_____

identify and apply relevant ethical principles: _____

_____

_____

_____

_____

choose the wisest option: _____

_____

_____

_____

state your justification: _____

_____

_____

_____

2. Apply each of the universal ethical principles reviewed in this chapter to the ethical issue of churning by brokers or investment advisors. Would each principle imply that the practice is right or wrong? Why?

a. egoism principle _____

_____

_____

_____

b. utility principle _____

_____

_____

_____

c. principle of rights _____

_____

_____

_____

d. principle of duties _____

_____

_____

_____

e. principle of virtues _____

_____

_____

_____

Digging Deeper

1. Go to the FTC's web site and find the application needed to obtain your free credit report.

2. Conduct a class project to find as many different kinds of credit card offers and applications as possible. Compare the ads and offers, paying special attention to the fine print. Which offers turn out to be the best deals? Which turn out to be the worst deals? Why?

3. Interview someone who works in a finance-related job. Ask the person about ethical issues and problems he or she has encountered. What kinds of legal and ethical guidelines are provided for the person to follow?

4. Conduct a survey among adults you know. Ask each person how many credit cards he or she has. Create a graph to show your results.

Personal Reflection

1. The most important ideas that I learned in this chapter were

2. This chapter made me think about

3. I would like to find out more about

4. One step that I could take to become a wiser manager of my personal finances is

8

Ethics and Computer Technology

Chapter Goals

After completing this chapter, you should be able to:

- Explain common ethical issues for computer users.
- Identify relevant ethical issues for students using computers for school.

Key Terms & Concepts

identity theft	copyright	computer viruses
phishing scams	piracy	plagiarism
spam	hacking	

What do you think?

Jake has a problem. He enjoys listening to music, watching movies, and playing computer video games, but he doesn't have much disposable income. He received an MP3 player for his birthday but can't afford to download many songs. He has a computer in his room on which he can play games and DVDs but doesn't have the cash to buy games and movies.

Jake's friend Maya offers a solution: Cut some corners. She tells Jake that he can download songs for free from a file-sharing site—and even shows him how. She also shows him web sites where he can download pirated versions of movies that are still in theaters and video games that are still popular items in stores. In addition, she and some friends have formed a "software club."

Whenever one of them buys computer software, that person makes copies for the rest of the group. And other than perhaps having to buy a few blank DVDs and discs on which to store the programs and files, none of this would cost Jake a cent.

Jake is thinking it over. Maya's offer sounds too good to be true, and he's fairly sure it is. He has heard that software piracy is illegal, but he's never heard of anyone getting caught and punished for it. Maybe it's one of those laws that is on the books but is never enforced. Jake doesn't want to get into trouble, but being able to get free movies, games, and music sounds very tempting.

What do you think?

The Apollo 11 space flight took place about 40 years ago. The mission marked the first time humans walked on the surface of the moon, one of the most important events of the 20th century. That space flight could not have taken place without major innovations in computer engineering and technology. Yet the computers and software programs used by NASA in the 1960s and 1970s are now considered primitive. A single home computer today is far more sophisticated and powerful than all of the computers on the Apollo spacecraft combined!

You live in a time of exploding technological growth. The inventions and ideas help people solve difficult problems and improve the quality of lives, but, at times, they also raise new ethical questions. In this chapter, you will investigate several ethical issues, questions, and problems associated with computers and new technologies.

You Decide

Read each of the following situations involving ethical decisions. After each statement, write *yes* or *no;* then briefly explain why you made that decision.

1. You have less than a week to complete your senior research project. You have been very busy participating in spring sports, working at a part-time job, enjoying your senior year, and making plans for life after graduation. You have not had much time left for schoolwork. But if you don't get a passing grade on this paper, you may not graduate with your class. A friend shows you a web site where you can buy research papers written by college students. Would you buy a paper?

Yes or No? _____

Why or why not? _____

_____

2. Instead of buying a paper, a friend suggests that you use the Internet to find articles and papers about your topic, then use the Copy and Paste functions to assemble a paper of your own. You can even cite the original documents as research sources. That way you end up with a complete paper and don't have to write more than a few original paragraphs. Would you follow your friend's advice?

Yes or No? _____

Why or why not? _____

_____

3. You find a web site that explains how to hack into your school's computer network. The site says that you can go into the school's system and play a prank, such as switching phone numbers or altering the times the bells ring to start and end class periods. Would you do that?

Yes or No? _____

Why or why not? _____

_____

4. A friend tells you in confidence that she has been spending hours every week instant-messaging a teenage boy in another state. Or at least that's who she thought it was. Now the messages are starting to get creepy. The person described what she was wearing yesterday and said he had followed her home from school one day without her knowledge. She's afraid that the messages are getting more threatening. But she makes you promise not to tell anyone, especially an adult. She is more afraid of getting in trouble at home if her parents find out what is happening. Would you break your promise and tell an adult?

Yes or No? _____

Why or why not? _____

_____

Personal Reflection

Researchers Peggy Bates and Margaret Fain surveyed students, looking for reasons for academic dishonesty. Their surveys and interviews found some common themes:

- Some students cheat or plagiarize in a desperate attempt to maintain high grades. They may be facing tremendous pressure from parents to get into the best schools or to get scholarships.

- Other students seem to think that cheating has become socially acceptable and, therefore, must be ethical.

- Some students are so overloaded with work, school, and family demands that they don't have time to complete their schoolwork without cheating.

- Other students view some courses as wastes of time and justify cheating on that basis.

- Some students don't seem to understand the deeper purposes of an education. They see school only as a series of obstacles on the way to a job. Cheating is one way around the obstacles.

- Other students cheat out of self-defense. They see other students cheating and begin cheating themselves to keep things fair.

- Some students have never been taught what actions constitute plagiarism.

Do you think that cheating in school can ever be justified by the reasons listed above or by any other reasons? Explain.

"We cannot live happily as human beings in the belief that our own actions don't matter."

—Alvin Toffler

Computer Ethics Issues for Users

Throughout history, advances in technology have often helped people to be more productive and to improve the quality of their lives. The earliest technological advances, such as the use of metals and the inventions of tools and the wheel, made it possible for humans to survive in a hostile environment. Later technologies, such as electricity, telephones, automobiles, and airplanes, made life more convenient and brought people from distant places together. Throughout human history, several patterns have emerged in the relationship between people, ethics, and new technologies.

One pattern has been that humans have a love/hate relationship with new technologies. People are both attracted to a technology's potential for good and frightened of its unknown potential consequences. However, in spite of people's fears, once new technologies are visualized, they usually are produced. For example, humans envisioned "horseless carriages" and "flying machines" many years before automobiles and airplanes were invented. A few people understood that the ability to transport people to distant places quickly would be essential as new societies sprang up around the world. Many more people were excited by the romance and adventure of traveling to new lands. However, some early skeptics of trains and automobiles warned that traveling at high speeds would damage people's internal organs. In the end, of course, trains and automobiles were built anyway, and the skeptics were quieted by reality.

Another pattern is that only *after* new technologies are introduced into a society are the ethical implications of the technologies understood. For example, early researchers into the nature of the atom suspected that their findings would revolutionize life on Earth. However, they could not have known all of the ethical questions that their research would later raise.

A third pattern in human history is that the more potential new technologies have to be used for good, the more potential they also have to be used in harmful ways. Airplanes, for example, have helped humans see past their national, racial, and geographic barriers to better understand the common traits that all people share. On the other hand, airplanes also helped usher in modern warfare in which millions of civilians have been killed through air raids and bombings. Like all other technologies, airplanes themselves are not good or bad. It is how they are used that can be considered right or wrong.

A fourth and somewhat surprising pattern is that new technologies do not produce new ethical issues at all. Instead, the innovations simply force people to look at *old* ethical issues in new ways. After all, humans had been wrestling with the ethics of war long before airplanes were invented. And people were concerned about an individual's right to privacy long before computers came along.

Personal Data Collection

Some of the more frightening aspects of recent computer technology have to do with people's privacy rights. Every time people use credit cards, file insurance claims, order products online, receive speeding tickets, or enter hospitals, their personal information is entered into computer databases. Certain laws in existence should protect people from having that information used without their consent. Unfortunately, those laws have not kept pace with advances in

Learn More

Use the Internet to learn more about the piracy of music, movies, games, or software. Choose one interesting or useful fact to share with the class.

technology. Businesses and nonprofit organizations, for example, sometimes sell lists of their customers' names and addresses to other companies. In many states, those actions are legal, even without the customers' permission. Even more harm can be done when the stored information is not accurate. One recent study found that more than one-third of credit reports kept on Americans contained mistakes and inaccuracies.

Even when the businesses compiling the information do so accurately and ethically, computer hackers sometimes gain access to the information. One student hacker recently demonstrated that fact during a class presentation. After only a few hours of work on his home computer, the student produced his teacher's address, phone number, Social Security number, confidential financial credit report, telephone records, and driving record for the past five years.

Protecting people's privacy will become even more difficult as the number of companies collecting and needing access to information continues to increase. Already, several major financial data collection companies have been hacked into, resulting in millions of stolen financial records. Corporations and computer security specialists, some of them former hackers, work tirelessly to protect company computer networks. Their goal is to stay one step ahead of the hackers, who are just as determined to penetrate the new security programs.

Personal Identity Theft

One of the most serious ethical and legal problems in today's electronic age is personal identity theft. **Identity theft** occurs when someone steals another person's personal information, such as credit card account numbers and Social Security numbers, for personal financial gain. Often that information is used to open new lines of credit, allowing the thief to obtain cash and purchase goods and services. Some victims of identity theft are tens of thousands of dollars in debt by the time they find out anything is wrong. And while they may not be required to repay all of the money, their personal credit is often ruined, requiring years to get their financial lives back in order. Obtaining loans for mortgages, cars, or education is more difficult and frustrating because their credit reports now show them to be poor risks for lenders. These victims range from senior citizens to very young children. According to a recent news story, people have used the Social Security numbers of children as young as two and three to obtain credit cards and other loans.

To minimize your risk, check your personal credit report annually for any irregularities. The government Consumer Protection Agency also provides these tips:

- Use passwords on your credit accounts that others cannot easily guess.
- Be cautious about giving out personal information to anyone.

Attempts to get personal financial information using phone calls, the mail, or the Internet are called **phishing scams**. They are very common. Pay attention to what you put in your trash. Tear or shred personal papers and cut up discarded credit cards. Don't leave outgoing mail that contains personal information in your mailbox. Don't carry your Social Security card with you. Carry only the credit cards and identification that you need; leave the rest at home. Be skeptical about promotions, as they are often used by identity thieves to get information. Pick up new checks at the bank instead of having them mailed to your home.

Spam

Spam is a term given to unsolicited electronic advertisements. These ads arrive as unwanted e-mailed messages. According to a recent column by Ellen Goodman of *The Boston Globe*, spam now accounts for almost half of all Internet e-mails. Internet service providers (ISPs) can end up spending 10–15 percent of their gross revenues just to block these unwanted advertisements—as much as $10 billion per year across the industry.

ISPs, along with legislators, are trying various tactics to combat the problem. Goodman points out possible solutions. A "do-not-spam" list is in the works. Fines and other penalties may result for companies that send spam to computer users who have registered on the list. A Virginia state law provides jail time for anyone sending spam messages. Another law under consideration requires special labels on spam ads that make them easier to block.

There are obstacles to those reforms. Legally speaking, spam is difficult to define. How different is it from junk mail delivered by postal employees? Others argue that the messages are protected by freedom of speech guaranteed by the First Amendment to the U.S. Constitution. Even if antispam laws are passed, enforcing them will not be easy. The universal nature of the Internet makes it easy for spammers to set up shop in other countries where such laws would not apply and could not be enforced.

In the end, the answer may lie not in legislation, but in business. Computer users and network administrators can purchase relatively inexpensive software that will block most spam messages. Some of that software can be downloaded at no charge. However, spam purveyors are likely hard at work trying to create programs that will defeat the blocking software.

Copyright and Piracy

Copyright is a legal right granted to the creator, publisher, or distributor of a work. The right-bearer is understood to have exclusive control of the publication, production, sale and/or distribution of that work. The works can be musical, dramatic, artistic, literary, or electronic. Violations of copyright are illegal. This book, for example, is a copyrighted work. The copyright belongs to the publisher. Individuals wanting to copy portions of the book or to include portions in another work must request and receive permission from the publisher. Publishers frequently grant those permissions, sometimes at no cost, but copying or using the material without permission is illegal.

Piracy is the unauthorized and illegal reproduction, sale, distribution, or other use of copyrighted works. The term is generally used in relation to copyright violations involving movies, music, and software. Examples include making unauthorized copies of video games, CDs, or DVDs; downloading unauthorized music or other files; and making unauthorized copies of computer software. Prosecution can result from those illegal acts, which carry civil and criminal penalties. A student in a college ethics class once shared with his classmates that as a teenager, he had been convicted of illegally downloading music files. He and his parents were forced to pay a $10,000 fine even though his parents did not know what he had been doing.

Hacking

Hacking is the act of using computer equipment to "break into" the computer systems of others. Hackers use computers and modems the way burglars use lock picks to "get inside" other computers and networks. The hackers' goals may be as innocent as playing pranks and testing their skills against security systems. However, more sinister purposes can include accessing personal or confidential information, conducting corporate espionage, and carrying out terrorism.

Even if no property is damaged, hacking would seem to demonstrate a blatant disregard for the rights of others. However, many hackers view the act as a harmless game of trying to penetrate computer security programs. As hackers become more skilled at getting into computer systems, the owners of the systems create better security measures to keep the hackers out. In fact, many former amateur hackers now design computer security systems for a living.

Computer security expert Winn Schwartau maintains that not all hacking is illegal, unethical, or even harmful. He argues that the vast majority of hackers do much good. They are technicians, software designers, and programmers who create products and keep millions of networks running. In fact, Schwartau differentiates among many categories of hackers, including:

- Ethical Hackers (or White Hats), who are often hired by companies as consultants to test system security.
- Crackers, who break into computers and networks illegally.
- Hacker Gangs, organized groups that hack each other, web sites, and companies.
- Hactivists, those whose hacking goals are to further a social or political cause.
- Criminal Hackers (or Black Hats), professional criminal hackers whose goal is to make money and/or harm the interests of others.
- Cyber-Terrorist Hackers, violent extremists who use hacking as a tool to further their terrorist purposes.
- Nation-State Hackers, known as cyber-spies, who hack on behalf of the interests of their nation. Many countries, including the United States, hire hackers to defend government networks and computers and/or to actively infiltrate other governments' networks and computers.

"In the 21st century, survival will be a more complicated and precarious question than ever before, and the ethics required of us must be correspondingly sophisticated."

—Oscar Arias

Viruses

Computer viruses are programs designed to negatively affect other computers, usually by causing loss of information. Viruses are high-tech vandalism. These programs are often spread when they are hidden in other programs. The other programs are put onto computers, either by use of CDs or through e-mail via a network. The viruses go along for the ride and begin to spread and do their damage. Computer owners should buy security programs that identify, quarantine, and delete viruses. However, malicious computer programmers are involved in a continual contest to create viruses that can penetrate security systems.

The following actions can minimize your risk of "catching" a virus:

1. Purchase good antivirus software. Several quality programs are on the market; a local computer professional can recommend one.

2. Be cautious about opening e-mails, particularly e-mail attachments from strangers. However, some sophisticated viruses now disguise themselves as e-mail attachments from someone you know whose computer has been infected. The most likely way for a virus to infect a computer is through an e-mail attachment.

3. Do not download computer files from strangers. Be cautious about downloading files from friends for the same reasons. Some experts recommend that if you have to download a file, download it to a floppy disk or CD first, then use your antivirus program to scan it for viruses.

4. Be skeptical about e-mails that other people forward to you, as this is a prime tactic for spreading viruses. The name of the person forwarding it to you may not be legitimate, or the virus may be e-mailing itself this way.

5. Finally, since you can't guarantee that you will never get a virus, back up the data and files on your computer regularly. It does not take long to download everything onto a CD, an external hard drive, or another storage device. But you will have peace of mind knowing that you won't lose everything if the worst happens.

Internet Communications

One of the best features of the Internet is the many ways in which it has revolutionized interpersonal communication. While the telephone made global communication possible, logistics and expense limited its use. E-mails have no such limits. A person in China can send an e-mail to someone in Greenland and get an almost instant reply. Instant messaging, video cameras, and other refinements can make the process live.

Instant global communication is altering the political dynamics of the world. It is becoming more difficult for tyrannical dictators and regimes to keep their people enslaved through ignorance and propaganda. Knowledge has a way of opening doors to freedom and democracy.

However, this powerful instrument for good can also be used to cause harm and pain. Every day, sexual predators prowl Internet sites, discussion forums, and specialty services such as MySpace. Practiced at the art of disguising who they really are, predators are looking for vulnerable children and teens. These pseudorelationships often build and develop slowly over weeks and months as the predators steadily break down their victims' defenses and earn their trust, with the goal of eventually luring the victims to a meeting place. By the time some victims discover what is actually going on, their lives are in danger.

Ironically, law enforcement professionals also use the same electronic communication tools. Officers working in computer-related crime divisions pose as vulnerable teens, hoping to lure dangerous predators into the open, where they can be captured. While the law enforcement professionals have had many successes, currently there are far more predators than there are officers available to do this kind of work.

There are other ethical issues related to Internet communication that, while less frightening, still raise important moral questions. The sense of anonymity with e-communication presents concerns. Normal protective inhibitions seem to diminish. Teens may be tempted to use offensive and suggestive language that they would not use in normal conversations and relationships. They may send or post pictures of themselves, a behavior that predators are counting on.

When relationships are created by e-mail and instant messaging, a person may be tempted to bend the truth. One student explained her experiences by saying, "Most 16-year-olds on the Internet are actually 13. Everyone says they're good-looking and seem much cooler than they really are when you meet them."

Checkpoint

In your own words, summarize the ethical issues involved in each of these areas:

personal data collection _____
_____
_____

personal identity theft _____
_____
_____

spam _____
_____
_____

copyright and piracy _____
_____
_____

hacking _____
_____
_____

viruses _____
_____
_____

Internet communications _____
_____
_____

Consider Jake's decision about illegally downloading movies, music, software, and games. Here are some questions to discuss with your classmates as you think through the issues involved.

1. Why are laws passed to prohibit illegal copying of software and other electronic data?

_____

_____

_____

2. Who benefits from those laws? How?

_____

_____

_____

3. What would the consequences be if all of those laws were repealed?

_____

_____

_____

4. Realizing that the sole source of income for many creative people is royalty payments from sales of the works they create, would your opinion change if you were a musical recording artist or an independent software programmer?

_____

_____

_____

Personal Reflection

Which of the three ethical issues discussed in this section (collecting personal data, monitoring employees, or spamming) do you think represents the most serious ethical problem? Why?

Computer Ethics Issues for Students

Professor Donald M. McCabe is the founder of the Center for Academic Integrity at Duke University. In a recent study, McCabe reported that 87 percent of students surveyed admitted to cheating on written work and 70 percent to cheating on a test. Forty-nine percent collaborated with others on an assignment, 52 percent copied from someone, and 26 percent plagiarized. *Term paper mills*, clearinghouses where students purchase academic research papers, have existed for years, but the rise of Internet term paper sites and other electronic resources has made the practice of plagiarism more convenient and more common.

Plagiarism

Plagiarism is the act of taking work written or created by someone else and using it as one's own. It would be difficult to find anyone who does not understand that buying and using papers written by others constitutes plagiarism and cheating—and is ethically wrong. However, many students don't recognize that copying written material from Internet sites can also be a form of plagiarism.

For example, Rogelio has a research paper due in his history class. His assignment is to research Abraham Lincoln's motives for issuing the Emancipation Proclamation. Rogelio goes to his favorite Internet search engine and keys in *Emancipation Proclamation*. Almost instantly, a screen pops up, providing him with over a million relevant web sites and listing the 25 best matches for his search. Rogelio locates five academic papers about his topic, utilizes the Copy and Paste functions on his computer to lift various paragraphs of material from each of the papers, organizes and edits them to fit his outline, changes a few words for authenticity, puts his name on his creation, and prints the paper—an entire research paper in about an hour!

Rogelio may try to fool himself into thinking that what he did was research, but it was, in fact, plagiarism. And how he went about writing the assignment may not be noticed by a tired teacher with a stack of papers to grade. But the odds are good that he will get caught eventually. A growing number of high school teachers and college professors now employ specialized computer programs that check sentences and phrases in papers against huge databases of papers on the Internet. When the program finds a phrase in a paper that matches a phrase in the database, the instructor is alerted to check both documents to determine whether the phrase was plagiarized.

Even if some students are never caught plagiarizing, they know that cheating is ethically wrong. To claim that a work is your own when it is not is lying. While many cheaters assume that their actions are between them and their teachers, cheating primarily violates the rights of fellow students, especially those who work honestly. Cheating devalues the entire academic process, cheapening the grades and diplomas for which students work so hard.

Additionally, in the end, cheating is self-defeating. It robs students of the belief that they can be academically successful on their own; thus, the practice may become a habit. Every time a person cheats, it gets easier for him or her to cheat in the future and harder to act with integrity and honor. Sooner or later cheaters get caught. No one can fool all of the people all of the time. If the consequences don't come in school, they may well happen in the workplace. Many individuals have found themselves fired from jobs, their careers ended, when they gave in to the temptation to cheat. Resorting to cheating to achieve short-term goals can make your long-term goals impossible to attain.

Real-World Ethics

An annual survey of America's brightest teens by "Who's Who Among American High School Students" includes a question asking whether teenagers have cheated to pass exams. In the survey, 80 percent of the students admitted to cheating—an all-time high. Fifty-six percent said that they were motivated by "competition for good grades." Fifty-three percent said that cheating "didn't seem like a big deal."

©Digital Vision

Professor and researcher Donald McCabe surveyed almost 16,000 students at 31 top universities. Seventy-six percent of business majors admitted to at least one act of cheating on an important assignment. Nineteen percent confessed to cheating four or more times. Moreover, 68 percent of future doctors, 63 percent of future lawyers, and 57 percent of future teachers admitted to cheating on a test at least once.

Why does cheating in school matter? People who cheat in school are more likely to cheat in their business and professional lives. A few years ago, the Pinnacle Group found that 67 percent of high school students surveyed expected to inflate their expense accounts when they entered the business world. Fifty percent said they would pad insurance claims. Sixty-six percent expected to lie to achieve an important business objective.

Validating Information from the Internet

Conducting an Internet search on a topic can yield an enormous storehouse of information—some of it invaluable, and some if it of questionable validity. How do you evaluate information from the Internet when sources are anonymous and anyone can post information?

Mark Snyder, a technology consultant for Fortune 500 corporations, has reported that 43 percent of Internet sites utilized for academic and business research contain factual errors, misstatements, or lies. Think about that. Almost half of the web sites that you and your fellow students rely on as being accurate contain false and misleading information. Students assuming that all web site–based facts are true can end up looking silly and may receive a low grade on an important assignment.

The consequences for businesses can be even more costly. Corporations use research data to make important decisions, sometimes involving huge sums of money. A company might need information to determine the best location for a new factory, to choose a new supplier, or to decide when to release a product. Many businesses hire full-time researchers for that purpose. What would happen to a researcher's job if he or she obtained data that turned out to be false, costing a corporation millions of dollars?

What can you do to ensure that the information you find on the Internet is accurate? While you can never be 100 percent certain about the accuracy of every research fact you uncover, you can take some practical steps to maximize your chances of getting the facts right. Author Robert Harris recommends the CARS model for evaluating web site facts and information.

C—Credibility. What makes this source believable? How does this source know the information? Why should this source be believed over others? Warning signs include anonymous articles or web pages, clear lack of quality control, many negative reviews of the web site, bad grammar, and misspelled words. To test a site's credibility, check the author's identity and credentials. Is the author's name and biographical information provided? What is the author's position, job, or title? In addition, look for evidence of quality control. For example, make sure the information was obtained from other respected sources, such as books or journals with quality control processes.

A—Accuracy. Is the information up to date, factual, detailed, exact, and comprehensive? Indicators of lack of accuracy include documents with no dates, stereotypes and generalizations, old dates on information known to change rapidly, and one-sided views on issues. To test for accuracy, check timeliness, comprehensiveness, and intended purpose. Does the author tell the whole story or just the part that fits his or her purpose? What is the author's aim—to sell you something, to persuade you to agree with a point of view, or simply to inform you?

R—Reasonableness. Are the arguments presented balanced and reasoned? Symptoms of unreasonableness might include obvious fallacies (especially name-calling), exaggerations, and clear conflicts of interest. An example might be a corporate web site with links to research studies about how great the company's products are. To test reasonableness, check fairness, objectivity, moderateness, consistency, and world view. Are opposing arguments presented fairly? Is the information slanted toward one side or the other of an issue? Is the information believable? Does the information contradict itself, or is it logically consistent throughout? Does the author write from a narrow political or ideological position or from one that is more balanced and objective?

S—Support. Can this information be corroborated by other sources, and are those sources provided? Indications of poor support include numbers or statistics presented without identified sources, an absence of source documentation, and a lack of other sources that present the same information. To test for support, check source documentations and bibliographies. Are sources clearly identified? Check several to be sure they are valid. This is especially important when statistics are presented as evidence of fact. Are other research sources provided that back up and support the position given?

A process such as the CARS model requires some effort. But that extra work is essential if you want to have confidence in the facts you present. Otherwise, you may find yourself embarrassed when an instructor or a supervisor tells you that the information on which you based a report is not true.

Checkpoint

1. In your own words, explain the ethical issues involved in the following practices.

a. plagiarism _____

_____

_____

b. validating research information from the Internet _____

_____

_____

2. Paraphrase the main point of each step of the CARS model.

a. credibility _____

_____

_____

b. accuracy _____

_____

_____

c. reasonableness _____

_____

_____

d. support _____

_____

_____

What do you think now?

Reread Jake's story at the beginning of the chapter. Apply the following universal ethical principles to his decision. Decide whether each principle would imply that he should copy the music, movies, games, and software or that he shouldn't? Explain.

egoism principle _____

_____

utility principle _____

_____

principle of rights _____

_____

principle of duties _____

_____

principle of virtues _____

_____

Personal Reflection

Have you ever cheated on a school assignment or exam? If so, describe the situation. How did you feel about it then? How do you feel about it now? If you have never cheated, why do you think that is so? What kept you from cheating when you may have been tempted?

Summary

Common ethical issues for computer users include personal data collection, identity theft, spam, piracy, hacking, viruses, and Internet communication.

Computer-related ethical issues for students include plagiarizing and validating information from Internet sources.

Vocabulary Builder

Match the following terms to their definitions.

a. computer viruses

b. copyright

c. hacking

d. identity theft

e phishing scams

f. piracy

g. plagiarism

h. spam

1. _____ Attempts to get personal financial information using phone calls, the mail, or the Internet

2. _____ The act of taking work written or created by someone else and using it as one's own

3. _____ The act of using computer equipment to "break into" the computer systems of others

4. _____ A legal right granted to the creator, publisher, or distributor of a work

5. _____ Programs designed to negatively affect other computers, usually by causing loss of information

6. _____ The act of stealing from others personal information such as credit card account numbers and Social Security numbers for personal financial gain

7. _____ The unauthorized and illegal reproduction, sale, distribution, or other use of copyrighted works

8. _____ Unsolicited electronic advertisements

Reinforcement

1. Create a code of ethics for Internet communication, including principles and rules that you think should be required of everyone.

_____

_____

_____

_____

_____

_____

2. Reread the earlier section that provided tips for minimizing your risk of identity theft. Create a chart to show the areas where you feel most protected and the areas where you think you might be vulnerable. Write at least two actions you can take to further minimize your risk.

_____

_____

_____

_____

_____

_____

Thinking Critically

1. Apply the ETHICS model to Dave's situation.

Dave Cheng is in his first year of teaching computer classes at Lincoln High School. He has been frustrated because the school's computer labs are stocked with old, nearly obsolete software. Last month Dave ran across a computer magazine article about MegaTeach, a new tutorial program. The article said that MegaTeach was the best software ever written for teaching high school students how to use computers. Although MegaTeach was expensive ($300 per copy), Dave decided to order it for himself, sacrificing some of the money he had been saving for a new car.

When Dave tried out MegaTeach at home, he found it was every bit as good as the article had said. In his excitement, Dave showed the article and the software to his friend Arlene, a math teacher at Lincoln. Her reaction was discouraging. "Dave," said Arlene, "there are 20 computers in your lab. Buying this software for every computer would cost $6,000! The school can't afford to spend that kind of money right now. The school already has to buy new band uniforms and resurface the gym floor this year. If you request MegaTeach today, you won't get funding for a year or two! Why don't you order it now and just make 20 copies to use until the school buys legal copies? Don't tell anyone, but that's how I got the WhizMath computer software for my classes."

That night Dave sat at his kitchen table, thinking about his dilemma. His students could really benefit from MegaTeach. But by the time the school could afford to buy it, MegaTeach might be obsolete. Making the copies would be easy, but would it be right? The copyright statement on the software clearly said, "If MegaTeach is used on multiple computers, a separate copy of the software must be purchased for each computer used."

evaluate the problem: _____

_____

think through the options: _____

_____

_____

highlight the stakeholders: _____

_____

_____

identify and apply relevant ethical principles: _____

_____

_____

_____

_____

choose the wisest option: _____

_____

state your justification: _____

_____

_____

_____

2. Select an ethical issue relevant to computers and computer technology. Locate a web site about that issue and utilize the CARS model to evaluate the validity of the site and the information on it.

C: _____

_____

A: _____

_____

R: _____

_____

S: _____

_____

Digging Deeper

1. Survey students at your school about the topic of cheating. Create your own list of questions, but here are a few suggestions:

a. Have you cheated on a school assignment within the past week or month?

b. What is the most brazen attempt at cheating you ever saw?

c. What is the worst consequence you ever saw someone receive for cheating?

d. What situations or reasons, if any, truly justify cheating?

2. Collect several examples of spam and bring them to class to share and compare with classmates.

3. Find an Internet site that contains false or misleading information. Print a copy of your findings and bring it to class for discussion.

Personal Reflection

1. The most important ideas that I learned in this chapter were

2. This chapter made me think about

3. I would like to find out more about

4. One step I could take to make myself less vulnerable to identity theft is

9 Ethics and Human Resources

What do you think?

Julie works in the human resources department of a family-owned business that manufactures specialty parts for bicycles. Business has been good lately, and the company has been looking to hire more assembly line employees. Julie's close friend Bandu has been out of work and looking for a job. Julie suggests that Bandu complete an online employment application with her company. "I know the owner and can put in a good word for you," she tells him.

When Bandu's application comes through, Julie checks it over and sends it to the owner for final approval. The next day it is returned to her marked "Rejected." When Julie asks why, the owner seems uneasy. "What I'm about to tell you is confidential," he warns her. "This is a small company. We seem to be more comfortable and productive when we don't have too much diversity. That's been our policy in the past, and I don't see any point in changing things now."

Although he has lived in America for several years, Bandu was born in India. Julie knows that he is talented, smart, and hard-working. She enjoys her job and makes good money, but she is angry at the owner for discriminating against Bandu and is embarrassed that she has to tell her friend that he will not be hired. As Julie looks around the company, it dawns on her that there aren't many employees who are members of a racial or ethnic minority group. She wonders whether she should quit her job in protest, report this fact to someone, or keep her mouth shut and try to help Bandu find a different job.

What do you think?

You Decide

Read the following statements about ethics in the workplace. Decide whether you think each action is right or wrong; then explain your reasoning.

1. A company administrator gives a promotion to a relative or close friend even though another employee is more qualified.

Right _____ Wrong _____

Reasons _____

_____

2. A supervisor allows employees to tell off-color jokes and hang suggestive posters in the break room even though some female employees have reported being offended.

Right _____ Wrong _____

Reasons _____

_____

3. A supervisor implies that an employee has a better chance at a promotion if the employee will go out on a date with him.

Right _____ Wrong _____

Reasons _____

_____

4. The manager of Department G often yells at and threatens employees to make them more productive. As a result, Department G has the highest productivity in the company.

Right _____ Wrong _____

Reasons _____

_____

5. An insurance company has an unwritten policy of hiring pretty young women to be front desk receptionists so they will be the first company representatives that potential customers meet.

Right _____ Wrong _____

Reasons _____

_____

Ethical Issues in Human Resources

In most companies, the **human resources** department is responsible for personnel recruitment, hiring, and management. Consider for a moment how important that function is. The company's success depends on its employees. Hiring good employees depends on the actions of the staff in the human resources office. Unwise hiring decisions and inadequate employee training can cost businesses thousands, even millions, of dollars. Moreover, there are important legal and ethical issues that are especially relevant to human resource managers and staff members.

"Integrity requires us to do the right thing even when it costs more than we want to pay."

—Michael Josephson

Discrimination

Discrimination is the illegal treatment of a person or group based on prejudice. Federal laws protect people from acts of discrimination based on race, gender, age, religious beliefs, ethnic origin, marital status, or disabilities. (Some states and cities have additional laws prohibiting discrimination based on other factors, including sexual orientation.) In the workplace, laws against discrimination are supposed to guarantee everyone equal opportunities in hiring, pay, and promotions. However, that goal of real and full equality has proven difficult to achieve.

Most successful business leaders have come to understand the intrinsic value of diversity. In business, **diversity** is the goal of recruiting, including, and incorporating people of all types and backgrounds throughout the company. Researchers have consistently found that active diversity programs can help companies attract and retain talented employees, limit the costs associated with lawsuits, motivate employees to be more efficient and creative, open access to new markets, improve customer service and satisfaction, and reduce employee turnover and absenteeism.

The dual goals of increasing diversity and avoiding discrimination has led to laws requiring most businesses to practice **affirmative action**, that is, to take active measures to ensure equal opportunity in hiring and advancement decisions. The main original intent of federal affirmative action laws was to force companies that had practiced discrimination in the past to take additional steps to recruit minority applicants for hiring positions and consider minority employees for advancement. However, some critics have claimed that, over time, the practices have been extended to the point of creating **reverse discrimination**, the practice of giving jobs and promotions to less qualified minority applicants at the expense of better qualified members of majority groups. The courts have generally ruled in support of affirmative action policies and programs, but not to the point of generating reverse discrimination. The bottom line is that discrimination is wrong no matter whom it is practiced against.

Favoritism

The general principle should be that the most accomplished and qualified applicants get the jobs and the most accomplished and qualified employees get the promotions. You have already seen how discrimination can violate that principle. But what if the position goes to a person who is less qualified, not because of discrimination *against* anyone, but because partiality is being shown *toward* someone? That is called **favoritism**, and it is commonly expressed in a couple of ways.

Nepotism is the practice of granting workplace favoritism to one's relatives. For example, a vice president's daughter is promoted to supervisor when several other candidates are clearly more qualified. **Cronyism** is the practice of showing workplace favoritism toward one's friends. A supervisor gives a job to one of her golfing buddies, even though that person would not otherwise be considered as qualified for the position. What is wrong with these practices? Why shouldn't people in positions of power be allowed to give jobs and promotions to whomever they choose? After all, as the saying goes, "It's not what you know, it's who you know."

Nepotism and cronyism create many workplace problems. First, supervising a relative or close friend can result in a *conflict of interest*, a situation in which people's professional decisions and actions are influenced by their personal interests. Imagine being responsible for your brother's job performance evaluation. If you give him a positive evaluation, people may think you did so only because he's your brother. If you give him a negative evaluation, he may think you are being harder on him for the same reason. Either way, people now think they have reason to question your professional judgment. You may begin to question it yourself!

Moreover, the practices of cronyism and nepotism tend to lower overall employee morale. Other employees see that the hardest-working, most capable, and best-qualified people are not the ones who get the best jobs and promotions. That can lead the other employees to question the integrity of their managers and leaders—and even discourage employees from doing their best. After all, why try harder if the rewards are based on something besides job performance?

Finally, acts of favoritism can even have negative consequences for the people to whom the favoritism was shown. Imagine getting a big promotion at work, only to find out that the people who work with you and for you are convinced that you were given the position only because you are the president's cousin. You are not given the benefit of the doubt that other supervisors get. Your decisions and policies are criticized, second-guessed, and doomed to fail since no one seems to have faith in them. Your mistakes are magnified; your successes, ignored.

Workplaces function best when everyone believes that hard work and talent are the keys to advancement. Employee morale and job satisfaction are high when

"I don't know the key to success, but the key to failure is trying to please everybody."

—Bill Cosby

everyone believes that the playing field is level and that all employees have fair and equal opportunities.

Sexual Harassment

An especially insidious form of employment discrimination is **sexual harassment**, unwelcome physical or verbal behavior directed at employees because of their gender. There was a time, not all that many years ago, when women in the workplace were especially vulnerable to these types of abuses. Because of historic and ongoing gender discrimination, women were less likely to hold positions of authority or to be paid equitably for their work, resulting in a loss of power. In addition, few laws protected people from workplace harassment. It is important to understand that men can also be sexually harassed. However, the unfair distribution of power in the workplace left women at special risk. For many years, women were subjected to offensive actions, jokes, propositions, and even physical assaults.

Federal courts have since ruled that sexual harassment violates the protection given to all citizens by the Civil Rights Act of 1964. Two specific categories of sexual harassment have been identified and prohibited by the courts. The first is referred to as quid pro quo sexual harassment. **Quid pro quo** (a Latin phrase meaning "something for something else") harassment refers to situations in which sexual demands are directly tied to a person keeping his or her job or receiving a promotion or another job benefit. A classic example is a supervisor demanding sexual favors from a subordinate, either by threatening the subordinate's job or by promising a raise or promotion in return.

The other category of sexual harassment is referred to as **hostile environment**. In these cases, supervisors or coworkers use embarrassment, humiliation, or fear to create a negative climate that interferes with the ability of others to perform their jobs. One company was found liable because loading dock workers posted sexually oriented pictures around the workplace to intimidate the women employees. Another company was forced to pay damages for not putting a stop to inappropriate jokes and cartoons that were passed around the office. In fact, the hostile environment does not even have to be sexual in nature. Some companies have been fined for allowing a supervisor to berate, bully, and humiliate employees. The hostile conditions are met as long as the environment has the effect of interfering unreasonably with a victim's work performance or creating a hostile or intimidating workplace that affects the victim's psychological well-being.

While the government does investigate and prosecute allegations of sexual harassment, lawsuits in civil courts have had a huge effect on harassment in the workplace. Companies have paid millions of dollars in settlements and damages to victims of both forms of harassment. That has led other companies to invest in increased employee training in order to prevent future occurrences and limit corporate liability.

Drug/Alcohol Abuse

In one recent study of top U.S. corporations, company leaders were asked to list the most persistent and troublesome ethical problems that their businesses faced. The list included many issues that were not surprising, including employee theft, misuse of company computers, and environmental concerns. But the single most bothersome issue according to those surveyed was drug and alcohol abuse by employees.

"He who passively accepts evil is as much involved in it as he who helps to perpetuate it. He who accepts evil without protesting against it is really cooperating with it."

—Martin Luther King, Jr.

Why would substance abuse be singled out as the worst offense? For one thing, it is a leading cause of lost production due to employee sick time. Drug and alcohol abuse are also leading causes of employee accidents and injuries. It has a dramatic effect on employee turnover. When employees quit or lose their jobs, companies must pay to recruit, hire, and train replacements. Substance abuse drives up the costs of insurance that companies provide to their employees. In fact, some companies now have their workers drug-tested in order to obtain discounts on health and life insurance rates.

The U.S. government department that regulates safety in the workplace is the Occupational Safety & Health Administration (OSHA). According to OSHA, 65 percent of workplace accidents are caused by substance abuse and employees who abuse drugs file six times more workers' compensation claims for injuries on the job. The U.S. Department of Labor reports similar statistical evidence, as follows:

- Employees abusing drugs record 16 times more work absences than "clean" employees.
- 12.3 million adults are users of illicit drugs, and 9.4 million (77 percent) of those people work.
- An estimated 6.5 percent of full-time and 8.6 percent of part-time workers are illicit drug users.
- It is estimated that 6.2 percent of adults working full time are heavy drinkers.
- More than 60 percent of adults know someone who has reported for work under the influence of alcohol or drugs.

Learn More

Research issues related to workplace safety. Use the Internet or a library, but also talk to local business leaders and employees. What are common workplace safety hazards? What strategies do businesses use to promote worker safety?

Requiring employees to be drug-tested represents an important ethical issue, too. But different types of testing raise different questions. *Pre-employment drug testing* is designed to screen out job applicants who may abuse certain illegal drugs. One testing company reported that, on average, 3.3 percent of job applicants fail these screening exams. To save money, other businesses require *post-offer testing*, meaning that they don't test every applicant, but only those who are offered jobs. Many companies have policies that test employees who display symptoms or signs of drug abuse. This is referred to as *reasonable suspicion testing*. It is also routine for employees to be automatically tested after on-the-job injuries, a practice sometimes referred to as *post-accident testing*.

The most controversial type of drug testing is *random testing;* it subjects all employees to being tested with little or no advance notice. In other words, employees who do not abuse drugs, who do not display any signs of impairment, and who may have exemplary job histories must still endure the invasion of personal privacy required for drug tests. Even critics of random testing concede that there are occupations in which across-the-board testing could be justified on the grounds of public safety (for example, airline pilots, train engineers, police officers, and school bus drivers). But can random testing of restaurant dishwashers or telephone operators be justified on the same basis?

And what should be done with employees who do test positive for using illicit drugs? Should they be fired, or should companies offer to help those employees who want to overcome their addictions? There are business leaders on both sides of that debate, but the railroad industry presents an interesting contrast. Not so many years ago, the general policy was that railroad employees determined to be abusing drugs or alcohol were automatically fired. The result was that rather than seek help, employees with substance abuse problems tried to hide their addictions, which often made the problem worse. At some point, administrators noticed that the policy was not preventing drug and alcohol abuse as much as driving it underground, and a new guideline was established. Employees who failed drug tests would be fired, but those who self-reported their substance abuse problems would be offered medical assistance and counseling. As a result, instead of hiding their problems to keep their jobs, employees were more likely to ask for help, dramatically improving their chances of rebuilding their lives and becoming productive employees and citizens again.

Checkpoint

In your own words, explain the meanings of the following terms and concepts.

human resources _____

_____

discrimination _____

_____

diversity _____

_____

affirmative action _____

_____

reverse discrimination _____

_____

favoritism _____

_____

nepotism _____

_____

cronyism _____

_____

sexual harassment _____

_____

quid pro quo _____

_____

hostile environment _____

_____

Consider the story about Julie and Bandu at the beginning of the chapter. If Julie came to you for advice, what would you suggest she do? Explain your reasons.

_____

_____

_____

_____

Personal Reflection

If you were a corporate owner or executive, what would your policy be on employee drug testing? What would your policy be toward employees with substance abuse problems? Explain your reasons.

"The effects of our actions may be postponed, but they are never lost."

—Chinese proverb

Real-World Ethics

What are the most important leadership behaviors for business executives who want to promote ethical behaviors in their companies? A recent study by the American Management Association found that the character trait most effective in maintaining employee ethics was for the executives to keep their promises. When employees trust their leaders, the employees are more likely to be trustworthy themselves. In second place was keeping lines of communication open, followed by preventing retaliation against employees who report unethical or illegal actions and supporting ethical behavior within the company. When company leaders "walk the talk" (that is, they consistently do what they say), employees notice and hold themselves to higher standards, too.

©Getty Images/PhotoDisc

So far, the emphasis in this chapter has been on employee-related ethical issues. But there is more to managing human resources than simply dealing with those types of problems. Business administrators and supervisors have legal and ethical obligations to all of their employees. What are those obligations?

Employer Obligations

An **obligation** is a duty that one person has to another person. Something is owed. Someone is entitled to receive something from another person. An obligation to employees is very different from an employee benefit. A **benefit** is an inducement above and beyond a wage or salary that employers offer to employees. Businesses compete with one another for quality employees, and a generous package of benefits can help companies attract the best workers. But businesses do not necessarily owe their employees benefits. Benefits are *extras*. Very small businesses may not be able to afford them.

Obligations are not extras or perks. They represent legal and/or ethical requirements. All employees are entitled to the fulfillment of these obligations. Companies that do not meet their obligations have done something legally or ethically wrong. What do employers owe to all of their employees? What do all employees have a right to expect from their employers?

Early in American history, it was assumed that employees had few, if any, such rights. Men, women, and children worked long hours for very little money, often in dangerous surroundings. Employees who got sick or injured, as well as those who complained about unfair treatment, were fired and replaced. Those types of abuses helped lead to the establishment of trade unions. Powerless individuals banded together into powerful groups. Most businesses could not afford to replace all of their workers at once and were forced to give in to employee demands for basic human rights in the workplace.

Safe Workplace

One clear employer obligation is to maintain a safe working environment. Workers should be protected from conditions that could cause injury, illness, or death. On the other hand, some occupations are inherently dangerous. Based on the government's injury and mortality statistics, the most dangerous jobs include these:

- Mining
- Law enforcement
- Roofing
- Farming
- Taxi driving
- Fishing
- Construction
- Firefighting
- Installing electrical power
- Truck driving
- Logging/Timber
- Guarding armored cars

Clearly, some jobs are more dangerous than others, but even workers in those jobs are entitled to honest information about the risks and to whatever protective measures might be available. As mentioned earlier, OSHA regulates workplace safety and holds employers to certain safety standards. Businesses that violate those safety regulations can face heavy fines. In addition, workers injured in unsafe working conditions can sue the irresponsible employers. Most companies understand that it is in their own best interests to maintain a safe workplace.

Fair and Equitable Pay

Employers owe their employees fair pay for the work done, but determining specifically what constitutes fair pay is not easy. Fortunately for workers, employers compete for quality employees, and that competition helps to promote higher wages and salaries. Trade unions also utilize **collective bargaining**, negotiations between organized workers and employers to pressure companies to pay higher wages and offer more and better employee benefits.

On the other hand, the practice of outsourcing has been used effectively by some businesses to hold down employee pay. While the term originally meant "contracting with other companies to produce needed parts or supplies," **outsourcing** is now often used to describe the practice of contracting work to people and companies in other countries. For example, it is now common to call a customer service number and have the phone answered by someone in India or Pakistan. And a growing number of products proudly sold as "American made" are actually "American assembled" from parts manufactured in other countries.

Corporate leaders defend outsourcing by pointing out that consumers want the best possible products at the lowest possible prices. American workers may demand $20 per hour for a job that people in another country will do for $5 per day. This new global economy produces many benefits for many people, but some critics claim that it also serves to depress wages and salaries for people in certain jobs in wealthier nations.

Equal Opportunity

A cornerstone of contemporary business is the idea that all people should have equal opportunities to get jobs and promotions. U.S. laws and people's shared ethical principles require it. Unfortunately, in the real world, things are not always so simple or just. People are still discriminated against in hiring and promotion decisions because of their skin color, nation of origin, gender, religious beliefs, or age or because they have a disability. Some are denied jobs for which they are qualified. Others are hired but paid less than equally qualified coworkers. Some are denied equal opportunities for promotions and advancement in the company. Others are left unprotected from unfair treatment and abuse by supervisors or fellow employees. Still others are fired unjustly or are forced out early so the company doesn't have to pay retirement benefits, thereby saving money.

But those practices are illegal, and businesses found to have violated those laws can end up on the wrong end of very expensive lawsuits. While most of the lawsuits are filed and fought by individuals, in some cases, the suits are brought by groups of employees. One grocery store chain was forced to pay over $80 million to female employees who the court ruled had not been given opportunities equal to their male coworkers.

As expensive as the legal costs can be, the damage done to public relations can be even more expensive. Consumers do not tend to support businesses that they believe are discriminatory and unfair. Consumer groups and other special interest groups can organize **boycotts**, group agreements not to buy products or conduct business with certain companies to protest perceived injustices.

The Equal Employment Opportunity Commission (EEOC) is the federal agency charged with enforcing antidiscrimination laws and investigating allegations of job discrimination. The EEOC's mission statement includes the following:

> . . . the Commission will pursue fair and vigorous enforcement where there is any form or level of employment discrimination covered by the laws we implement. . . . Discrimination in the workplace on account of race, color, national origin, gender, age, religion or disability deprives the nation of the skills and talents needed to sustain economic growth and deprives families of the quality of life they deserve. Our Mission is to eradicate Employment Discrimination at the Workplace.

Critics of the EEOC have complained of inefficiency and tardiness in following through with investigations. But consider how big a job the agency faces. The agency is charged with protecting rights to a fair and nondiscriminatory workplace for all Americans working in all businesses and professions.

Respect

One worker summed up the importance of respect in the workplace by explaining how he felt about his job. "My employer treats me with all the dignity and respect of a shovel," he said. "They bought me as cheaply as they could; they use me up every day to the breaking point; and when I complain, they remind me that they can replace me with another shovel anytime they want to!"

Employers have an ethical obligation to treat their employees with respect. The idea was probably summed up best in Immanuel Kant's principle of *respect for persons*, which you learned about in Chapter 2. People should always treat others as ends or goals and never use them as a means only. To treat someone as a *means only* is to use them as a tool to get something. It is to use them in a way that harms their interests while furthering the other person's interests. It is to exploit them; to seek win-lose strategies. Kant maintained that that behavior is always unethical because it treats people as less than persons; it dehumanizes them.

If you treat people as *ends or goals in themselves,* you act in ways that further their interests as well as your own. You seek win-win strategies. The principle does not mean that you can never use each other, only that you must always use each other in ways that are mutually beneficial and not exploitive.

Perhaps nowhere is this principle more tested and strained than in the workplace. Employers use employees to make money. Employees use employers to make a living and to afford a satisfactory standard of living. But to avoid exploitation, everyone must remain committed to maintaining win-win relationships. Employers who exploit and abuse their employees to gain short-term profits are not fulfilling this obligation.

Unfortunately, too many employers still seem to fail to understand this principle, perhaps under the false belief that treating employees harshly will make them work harder. A recent study of workplace ethics by the Ethics Resource Center asked employees to list types of misconduct that they had observed in the workplace. The survey ranked abusive or intimidating behavior toward employees as the most common type of misconduct that employees had witnessed.

Exploitation and abuse may sometimes yield short-term profits, but that money is soon lost when frustrated employees leave and new employees must be hired and trained to replace them. Wise company administrators understand that treating employees with respect and fairness is essential to the long-term success

"If you want to succeed, you should strike out on new paths rather than travel the worn paths of accepted success."

—John D. Rockefeller, Jr.

of the organization. One employee summed up the way her company treated her by saying:

> They really do care about me as a person, not just as a tool. They care about my goals and aspirations and support my efforts to achieve them. The company helps pay my tuition expenses to further my education. They support me as a mother, understanding that I sometimes need more flexible working hours. They ask me what the company can do to help me do my job better. They pay me fairly and give me opportunities to earn raises and bonuses. Why would I ever want to work anywhere else?

Ethics & Law

What should an American company conducting business in another country do when that nation's laws conflict with U.S. laws? In 1996, the U.S. Congress passed the Helms-Burton Law, which strengthened economic sanctions against Cuba that had been in place since 1961. In 2006, a group of American business executives met to conduct trade with Cuban officials, in violation of this law, at an American-owned hotel in Mexico. The hotel obeyed a U.S. government request to expel the Cubans. However, Mexico and Cuba are allies and trading partners. The Mexican government was outraged and threatened the hotel with a fine of half a million dollars. The hotel managers pointed out that if they had refused the U.S. request, the hotel's corporate owners could have faced legal difficulties at home. What do you think the hotel should have done?

Checkpoint

Explain each of these concepts in your own words.

safe workplace _____

_____

fair and equitable pay _____

_____

collective bargaining _____

_____

outsourcing _____

_____

equal opportunity _____

_____

boycotts _____

_____

respect _____

_____

What do you think now?

Reread the story about Julie and Bandu at the beginning of the chapter. Most business leaders would maintain that discriminating against people in hiring or promoting is bad for business. Explain three ways that practicing job discrimination could actually harm a company's profits and success.

_____

_____

_____

Personal Reflection

If you have a job or have had one in the past, explain how well (or how poorly) your employer fulfilled its obligations to you as an employee. (If you have not had a job, interview someone who has and record his or her comments.)

safe workplace

fair and equitable pay

equal opportunity

respect

Summary

Ethical issues relevant to human resources include discrimination, favoritism, sexual harassment, and drug and alcohol abuse.

Employers have certain legal and/or ethical obligations to their employees, including maintaining a safe workplace, providing fair and equitable pay, giving all employees equal opportunities in hiring and promotions, and treating employees with dignity and respect.

Vocabulary Builder

Match the following terms to their definitions.

a. affirmative action
b. benefit
c. boycott
d. collective bargaining
e. cronyism
f. discrimination
g. diversity
h. favoritism
i. hostile environment
j. human resources
k. nepotism
l. obligation
m. outsourcing
n. quid pro quo
o. reverse discrimination
p. sexual harassment

1. _____ The department responsible for the recruitment, hiring, and management of personnel
2. _____ A duty that one person has to another person
3. _____ The goal of recruiting, including, and incorporating people of all types and backgrounds throughout the company
4. _____ A group agreement not to buy products or conduct business with a certain company to protest a perceived injustice
5. _____ An inducement above and beyond a wage or salary that employers offer to employees
6. _____ Negotiations between organized workers and employers to pressure companies to pay higher wages and offer more and better employee benefits
7. _____ The practice of contracting work to people and companies in other countries
8. _____ The practice of giving a job or promotion to someone less qualified because partiality is being shown toward that person
9. _____ The practice of giving jobs and promotions to less qualified minority applicants at the expense of better qualified members of majority groups
10. _____ The practice of granting workplace favoritism to one's relatives
11. _____ The practice of showing workplace favoritism toward one's friends
12. _____ The practice of taking active measures to ensure equal opportunity in hiring and advancement decisions
13. _____ A type of harassment in which embarrassment, humiliation, or fear are used to create a negative climate that interferes with the ability of others to perform at their jobs
14. _____ A type of harassment in which sexual demands are directly tied to a person keeping his or her job or receiving a promotion or another job benefit
15. _____ Illegal treatment of a person or group based on prejudice
16. _____ Unwelcome physical or verbal behavior directed at employees because of their sex

Reinforcement

1. Create a series of company policies to prohibit discrimination, favoritism, and sexual harassment. Include an explanation of the consequences of those actions and provide employees with instructions for reporting violations and seeking help if they are victimized.

_____

_____

_____

2. Assume that you are an administrator. Write a company statement to employees, outlining the company's obligations to employees and detailing how those obligations will be fulfilled.

_____

_____

_____

Thinking Critically

1. Apply the ETHICS model.

You work at a retail store in the mall. Your good friend Karen works there, too. Lately, she has seemed unhappy and uneasy at work and has been missing work more than usual. You have tried to be supportive without being nosy, but it's obvious that something is bothering her. One day at lunch, she breaks down and tells you that the store manager has been sexually harassing her. But she makes you promise not to tell anyone. Her family is going through a tough time financially, and they are depending on the money she makes. "The manager's just a creep," she tells you. "I won't give in to him, but I'm not going to quit because of him."

The store you work for is part of a large national chain, and the company handbook contains very clear instructions for reporting harassment, including a national 800 number to report such abuse. The policies promise to protect harassment victims from any retaliation or punishment. What should you do?

evaluate the problem: _____

_____

think through the options: _____

_____

_____

highlight the stakeholders: _____

_____

_____

identify and apply relevant ethical principles: _____

_____

_____

_____

_____

choose the wisest option: _____

_____

state your justification: _____

_____

_____

_____

2. Corporate administrators have an obligation to stockholders to maximize profits by carefully managing personnel costs. But these company leaders also have an ethical obligation to pay employees fairly and equitably and to offer benefits that will help attract quality employees. Write a one-page essay in which you explain how, as an administrator, you would try to balance those two responsibilities.

_____

_____

_____

Digging Deeper

1. Interview someone who works in the human resources department of a local business or corporation. Ask the person about one of the ethical issues discussed in this chapter, as well as about how the company he or she represents fulfills its obligations to employees.

2. Choose one specific type of discrimination (racial, gender, age, disability, religious, and so on). Use the Internet and other resources to research its history. Pay special attention to relevant antidiscrimination laws.

3. Survey people at your school. Ask them what they believe are the most important obligations that employers have to employees. Compile your findings with those of your classmates to determine which obligations seem most important overall.

Personal Reflection

1. The most important ideas that I learned in this chapter were

2. This chapter made me think about

3. I would like to find out more about

4. One step that I could take to protect myself from discrimination or sexual harassment is

10

Ethics for Employees

What do you think?

Moira recently graduated from college and landed her first corporate job. She works as an administrative assistant for a company that manufactures home decorations. On the job only four months, Moira feels as though she is already starting to lose her idealism about business. She has heard of many instances of employee theft and has even witnessed a couple of occurrences. She has observed employees coming to work intoxicated—even sneaking drinks at work. She has seen employees routinely arrive late for work and sneak out early. Fifteen-minute breaks and 30-minute lunches often end up lasting twice as long. Employees routinely use their computers for sending and receiving personal e-mails, shopping online, checking horoscopes and the weather, even gambling. And all of that is happening in just her department!

The department manager is very laid-back. Moira has tried to talk with him about the problem, but he seems unable or unwilling to confront the problems. It appears to Moira that he wants the employees to like him, and the employees are taking advantage of that. Moira is growing more and more frustrated. She prides herself on being a dependable, hard worker, and she took this job assuming that the other employees would be that way, too.

Moira is tempted to give up and join the other employees, getting paid for doing as little as possible. But she knows she wouldn't respect herself. She is tempted to go over her manager's head to his supervisor and complain about the problem. But that would alienate her supervisor and the other employees. She has not been at the company long enough to request a transfer, and quitting her job after four months doesn't seem like a wise career move. She is sitting at her desk one afternoon, wondering what she should do.

What do you think?

You Decide

You are a supervisor managing eight employees. The company has announced that layoffs are coming, and you must decide which employees to cut first. Rank the following employees from #1 (most valuable) to #8 (least valuable).

_____ This employee is talented and energetic, but uses crude and offensive language. Coworkers and customers have complained.

_____ Although unattractive in appearance, this employee is very dependable when you need something done. This person is always on time, is rarely absent, and never fails to follow through on a project.

_____ This employee works hard, but has been caught taking office supplies and company products for personal use.

_____ This employee is one of the most honest people you've ever known, although not terribly talented. You have never known this person to intentionally lie. You would trust this person with your personal bank account number, but not with your most important sales account.

_____ This employee is a follower. When others are working hard and being productive, this person is doing the same. But when others are wasting time or engaging in unethical conduct, this person joins in.

_____ This employee is an average worker with a lot of potential, but rarely seems to have much motivation. Although very smart and good with people, this person is frequently late and has the most absences in your department.

_____ This employee makes friends easily with coworkers and customers, but has a serious drinking problem.

_____ This employee never seems to make a mistake. Reports and documents are painstakingly written and errorless. But you recently caught the employee gambling online using a company computer.

Personal Reflection

Take a moment to reflect about your rank order of employees, looking for overall patterns. What character traits did you seem to value most? What traits did you seem to have the least patience for?

Most:

Least:

Ethical Violations by Employees

Ethics is a growing concern in today's workplace. Executives and managers in corporations all across the country are emphasizing the need for their workers to be ethical people. More than 85 percent of the largest corporations in America currently have written codes of ethics for their employees to follow. (A *code of ethics* is a written set of ethical guidelines that workers are expected to follow.) Many companies are also investing in resources such as ethics training programs and ethics hotlines to give employees guidance when facing ethical decisions in their jobs. Why are businesses going to this much trouble over ethics?

One reason is that many businesses have found that unethical actions by employees can be expensive. American companies lose billions of dollars in profits each year due to actions such as employee theft, abuse of sick time, and drug and alcohol abuse in the workplace. In addition, corporations are often held legally responsible for the actions of their employees. That means that companies can be sued when their employees act in unethical and illegal ways.

Employee Theft

The security director of a large retail store was explaining the new security system being installed there. He mentioned that the system cost over $350,000. A listener commented on how much money the store must be losing to shoplifters for such an investment to be justified. The security director shook his head sadly and said, "Our customers are fine. Our employees are stealing us blind!"

Each year employee theft costs the average American retail store nearly twice as much money as shoplifting does. Employees have increased access to products. They know more about store security procedures and ways to evade them. Employees may frequently be left unsupervised in the store while customers rarely are.

There are other types of employee theft, as well. Workers have been known to steal office supplies, equipment, cash, phones, computers, even company vehicles. The employees who get caught usually face company discipline. Many people have lost their jobs (even their careers) because they gave in to the temptation to take something that did not belong to them.

Wasted Time

According to one recent survey, the typical American worker spends an average of seven hours each workweek intentionally doing nothing productive. If that finding is accurate, it means that employees waste almost an entire day each week, in essence, getting paid for doing nothing. That practice can be viewed as another form of employee theft. How would you feel about wasted time if you owned a business? Wouldn't you do everything you could to make sure your employees worked hard and remained productive?

Some companies are doing everything they can. It is now fairly routine for companies to monitor telephone calls that their employees have with customers. Courts have ruled that phones, computers, and e-mails belong to the company, not the employee, so businesses are reading employee e-mails and monitoring what web sites workers access. Some businesses even monitor computer keystrokes to measure worker productivity, allowing occasional timed breaks to go to the bathroom. Employees exceeding the allotted minutes for bathroom breaks may be reprimanded.

While the desire to maintain a high level of productivity is understandable, employee rights advocates have criticized some of those practices as extreme and dehumanizing. The courts have ruled that the U.S. Constitution implies an individual's basic right to privacy. Do employees shed those rights when they go to work each day? If not, how can employers ensure that employees are behaving appropriately and remaining productive?

Misuse of Technology

A growing problem in the workplace is the misuse of computers, copiers, phones, and other technological equipment. One reason that many companies monitor employee phone calls is that too many employees use those phones for lengthy personal (even long-distance) calls. Other businesses complain that workers are using company copy machines for large personal copying projects in order to save ink on their home copiers.

Many companies describe the biggest problem as the misuse of company computers. You may remember an interesting fact mentioned earlier in this book. The number one shopping day of the year in the United States is the day after Thanksgiving, when many workers are on a holiday break. But the top *online* shopping day of the year is the Monday after Thanksgiving. That means a large number of employees make the conscious decision to wait until they get back to work to do their Internet shopping. Consider the combined thousands, perhaps millions, of hours of unproductive time that represents and the amount of money employers across the nation are losing on just that one day!

Another common computer-related misdeed involves other inappropriate web sites. Online gambling is a rapidly increasing phenomenon. For some people, the convenient access leads to addictive gambling, and they take the addiction with them to work. An even bigger problem for employers is online pornography. It has been estimated that between 50 and 80 percent of all Internet web sites contain some explicit sexual content. In addition to lost productivity, employees visiting sexually explicit web sites may also create conditions that can lead to sexual harassment allegations and lawsuits. The company can be found legally liable for not preventing the situations from occurring.

A corporate **trouble-shooter** is someone hired to solve specific problems. A trouble-shooter for an international corporation once spoke of his most unusual case. The corporation's security director had reported that employees were accessing sexually explicit web sites at an alarming rate. The company feared legal problems if the problem persisted, so the security director asked for the trouble-shooter's help in resolving the problem. Together the two men implemented a computer tracking system that would monitor every web site visited on the company's computers. A stern memo was sent to all employees, warning of the dire consequences of getting caught accessing inappropriate materials online. According to the trouble-shooter, the first person snared was the security director! He was caught by the very system he helped to develop, and his career was over.

While the problems of employee misconduct are serious and more common than they should be, it is important to keep in mind that most workers are good, honest people. Most employees don't steal, they give an honest day's work, they don't abuse drugs or alcohol, and they treat their supervisors and coworkers with respect. They are the employees businesses are looking for in job interviews. The unethical employees are simply too expensive to keep around.

Checkpoint

In your own words, explain what main issues are involved in the following employee misdeeds and why those issues are important to employers.

employee theft _____

_____

wasted time _____

_____

misuse of technology _____

_____

What do you think now?

Reread Moira's scenario at the beginning of the chapter. If she came to you as a friend seeking advice, what would you suggest she do? Why?

_____

_____

_____

_____

_____

Personal Reflection

Thinking about a job you have had, list three unethical actions that you saw other employees do. If you have not had a job, ask someone who has and write down his or her experiences.

©Digital Vision

When explaining why they choose to act ethically at work, most employees describe personal motivations. Recently, about 100 employees of businesses of various sizes were asked to complete an anonymous survey. They were asked whether being an ethical person in the workplace was important to them and why. Ninety-six percent of the respondents said that being an ethical person in the workplace was important to them, giving the following reasons. Which ones seem to reflect the way you might have answered the question?

Top 10 Reasons for Being Ethical in the Workplace

10. I want my family and friends to be proud, not ashamed, of my actions.
9. Ethics is more important than money. It's best to earn money honestly.
8. Acting ethically helps me avoid negative consequences such as ugly fights over power and money, expensive lawsuits, and unsafe products that could harm other people.
7. Ethical people tend to attract other ethical people, and I want to work with ethical customers and coworkers.
6. I believe in treating others the way I want to be treated, and I want to be treated ethically.
5. Acting ethically helps me earn the respect of others. It shows that I have respect for myself and others.
4. I want to do my part to make the world a better place, to be a role model for others. I don't want to just "go with the flow" and conform to unethical standards around me.
3. Acting ethically makes me feel like I'm a good person. It is helping me become the kind of person I want to be.
2. Ethical behavior is good for business. It gains the trust of customers, so they keep coming back. It also helps my company become more orderly and efficient.
1. The workplace is not separate from the rest of my life. I believe that people who act unethically in business act the same way in the rest of their lives. I want to be a good person in all aspects of my life.

> "Never fear the want of business. A man who qualifies himself well for his calling, never fails of employment."
>
> —Thomas Jefferson

Character Traits of Excellent Employees

You may remember from Chapter 2 that an *ethical virtue* is a character trait of a good person or a good life. Examples include honesty, generosity, caring for others, and courage. Business leaders look for those same kinds of virtues when making hiring and promotion decisions. Employees who consistently exhibit these virtues are often rewarded with promotions, opportunities, and raises. On the other hand, workers in whom those virtues are absent may be disciplined or fired or may spend the rest of their careers wondering why they can't seem to get ahead at work.

Honesty

The core of personal ethics is **honesty**. People who are consistently honest are perceived as being trustworthy. Others recognize that these people can be counted on—that they can be entrusted with sensitive, even confidential, information. What is honesty? The best definition may come from the courts—"to tell the truth, the whole truth, and nothing but the truth." Interestingly, those three parts of the traditional legal oath are not quite the same and are perceived in different ways.

The honesty violations that are generally perceived as being most serious are related to the phrase *nothing but the truth*. People often refer to that kind of violation as *lying*. That means a person says that something is or was when, in fact, it is not or was not. An employee injured in a fall at home lies, claiming that the accident occurred on the job, in the hope of getting better medical coverage or filing a fraudulent lawsuit. A manager tells slanderous lies about an employee to get that person fired so the job can go to the manager's friend. The consequences of that type of lying are usually severe because most people view that level of dishonesty as especially egregious.

The middle level of dishonesty concerns the phrase *to tell the truth*. These violations often involve a person not reporting something that he or she has an obligation to report. An employee becomes aware that the company is disposing of toxic wastes dangerously and illegally, but she doesn't report that information to anyone. A worker sees another employee being bullied and abused by a supervisor, but he keeps that knowledge to himself.

The level of dishonesty generally considered to be the least serious involves the third part of the oath, telling *the whole truth*. These violations are about not being forthcoming, about demonstrating a lack of openness. A police officer catches you speeding and pulls you over. When she tells you that she clocked you at 20 miles per hour over the speed limit, would you add that you also ran a red light? Should you? A coworker asks if you like his very expensive new suit. You reply honestly that you do. But should you also mention that the suit fits as though it is a size too small?

Integrity

Integrity is faithful adherence to a strict personal ethical code. Integrity implies consistency. It means being the same good person through and through. It means sticking to the truth and sticking up for one's principles no matter what the consequences. On the other hand, if you have ever known anyone who seemed to be a different person when someone else was around, then you know what integrity is not.

Integrity sometimes has to be its own reward, for it is not always rewarded by others. Pressures from peers, coworkers, and supervisors to take the easier path can often be very strong. The consequences of that easier path may seem better, at least in the short term. But people of integrity see a bigger picture and have the strength of character to shrug off such distractions and to continue to stand up for what is right, true, fair, and just.

Not all employers seek employees who display honesty and integrity. Some managers and administrators, perhaps motivated by greed and short-term thinking, are less than ethical themselves and may prefer the same in their employees. That is one reason why employees should be just as selective about whom they choose to work for as employers are about whom they hire. Few workplace situations are as miserable as being a person of integrity trying to succeed in a dishonest company.

Industriousness

To be **industrious** is to consistently demonstrate perseverance and hard work. If employers have an obligation to give a full day's pay for a day's work, then employees have the corresponding obligation to give a full day's work for a day's pay. Top workers demonstrate personal initiative, doing more than expected and looking for opportunities to do more.

This character trait requires a great deal of maturity and the wisdom to think long-term. It is not easy to keep working hard when others are doing much less—and may be getting paid the same or even more. For that reason, the workplace can sometimes seem unfair to industrious people, at least in the short term.

But the long-term rewards of industriousness can be great. Hard work and dedication get noticed. Since those qualities are not as common as managers might like, industrious employees tend to become very valuable to their employers. There is an old saying that the cream always rises to the top, and industrious employees are often the first to be considered for new opportunities and promotions.

"Sloth makes all things difficult, but industry, all things easy."

—Benjamin Franklin

Respect

Respect is the willingness to show consideration and appreciation for others. It means showing proper deference to a supervisor. Respect involves demonstrating consideration for coworkers and customers. Respectful people do not treat others abusively, dishonestly, rudely, or manipulatively. Being respectful means treating people as persons, not as tools, problems, or obstacles.

Someone once said that respect is best demonstrated by how you treat people who you don't think can help you. It is natural, even clever, to act respectful toward a supervisor who has the authority to fire or promote. But how many people go out of their way to act respectful toward people who are lower on the corporate ladder?

Legendary businessman Sam Walton founded Wal-Mart, the highly successful chain of discount retail stores that revolutionized American business, which made him one of the wealthiest people in the world. Walton possessed many character traits that led to his success, but few traits endeared him to his workers as much as the respect with which he treated them. Walton often traveled from store to store, encouraging his employees, and it was said that he knew the names of all of his store managers, as well as the names of their spouses! Imagine a person that busy taking the time to study the names of the people who work for him. That appreciation and respect for others was an important part of Walton's success.

Loyalty

Loyalty means faithful allegiance to a person, an organization, a cause, or an idea. One person might be loyal to friends or family members. Another might by loyal to his or her school or teammates. Still others might demonstrate loyalty through devotion to their religious faith, their country, or their ethical principles.

But in the context discussed here, loyalty refers to a company or an employer, and there are some important restrictions to that.

This character trait of excellent employees is not a blind loyalty that ignores or covers up wrongdoing. It is not unquestioned allegiance to coworkers, a supervisor, or even a company president. This ethical virtue is not a matter of "my company, right or wrong." The loyalty is not to people, but to the highest values and principles of the organization.

Few professions value loyalty as highly as law enforcement. After all, officers depend on one another for their lives. The unique demands of the job create a very close bond among law enforcement professionals. With that bond comes a high expectation of loyalty. Officers who witness illegal or unethical actions by other officers often feel torn. They know that telling the truth is the right thing to do and that they are obligated to do so. But they do not want their peers to consider them disloyal.

Loyalty should be highly valued in law enforcement. However, it is not simply a matter of allegiance to fellow officers. The higher, more important loyalty is to the ideals for which the profession stands. The true acts of disloyalty are by those who violate laws and ethical standards. Those reporting such abuses are, in fact, demonstrating the highest level of loyalty.

Ethics & Law

Occasionally, workers find out that their coworkers or employers are acting unethically and even illegally. Those workers then face the difficult decision of whether to blow the whistle. **Whistle-blowing** is the act of reporting unethical or illegal actions by one's superiors or peers to authorities or to the media. Blowing the whistle on one's own company requires a great deal of courage. Whistle-blowers are sometimes viewed as traitors by their employers and coworkers. They are often punished or fired even though state and federal laws protect whistle-blowers from retaliation.

Whistle-blowing cases can be difficult to resolve. Businesses often deny the charges made by whistle-blowers. The public is left unsure of whom to believe. After all, not all charges made by whistle-blowers are true. There are cases in which angry employees made up false allegations to embarrass their companies. Sometimes whistle-blowers simply get the facts wrong and make inaccurate assumptions. However, there are many cases in which the whistle-blowers' charges are proven to be correct. Actions by whistle-blowers can force businesses to change their policies, admitting that their actions were, in fact, unethical or illegal.

Whistle-blowers have saved lives by revealing dangerous products. They have saved taxpayers billions of dollars by speaking out against corrupt practices between businesses and government agencies. They have brought wrongdoers to justice by courageously testifying against their own companies in courtrooms. Are those results worth risking one's job for? Many whistle-blowers think so.

There is no secret to developing those kinds of virtues and becoming a good person and employee. The ancient Greek philosopher Aristotle explained the process almost 2,400 years ago. A dishonest person can become an honest person by being honest just one time when it isn't easy to do so. The person must then commit to doing it again—then again and again. Over time, honesty will become a habit. Once ingrained as a habit, honesty becomes part of an individual's personal character, part of his or her personal identity. This process works for all ethical virtues. Just decide what kind of person you want to be and act that way until you're there! But be patient with yourself when you experience setbacks. The only failure is to quit trying.

Checkpoint

Explain what each of these employee virtues means to you.

honesty _____

_____

integrity _____

_____

industriousness _____

_____

respect _____

_____

loyalty _____

_____

What do you think now?

Reconsider Moira's story at the beginning of the chapter. Assume that you are hired to replace the current ineffective department manager. What three steps could you implement to improve the efficiency and morale of the department?

_____

_____

_____

_____

_____

_____

Personal Reflection

Which one of the employee virtues do you see as your biggest strength? Which do you see as your biggest weakness? Explain how you could turn that weakness into another area of personal strength.

Summary

Common ethical violations by workers include employee theft, wasted time, and misuse of company equipment and technology. Employees who are guilty of those offenses often find the consequences to be very serious, including the loss of jobs and even careers.

Character traits of top employees include honesty, integrity, industriousness, respect, and loyalty. Employees exemplifying those qualities are often rewarded with increased responsibilities, opportunities for advancement, and better pay.

Vocabulary Builder

Match the following terms to their definitions.

a. honesty

b. industrious

c. integrity

d. loyalty

e. trouble-
shooter

f. respect

g. whistle-
blowing

1. _____ The act of reporting unethical or illegal actions by one's superiors or peers to authorities or to the media
2. _____ A person hired by a company to solve specific problems
3. _____ The character trait of consistently demonstrating perseverance and hard work
4. _____ The character trait of consistently telling the truth, the whole truth, and nothing but the truth
5. _____ The character trait of maintaining adherence to a strict personal ethical code
6. _____ The character trait of maintaining allegiance to a person, an organization, a cause, or an idea
7. _____ The character trait of showing consideration and appreciation for others

Reinforcement

1. Imagine that you are ready to invest a lot of money to start your own business. Your plan is to hire five employees to help get the company off the ground. You know that your success or failure will depend, as much as anything else, on the quality of work of those five people. First, list character traits that you would want in the people you hire. Then list character traits that you would consider unacceptable in new employees.

preferred employee character traits _____

_____

_____

_____

unacceptable employee character traits _____

_____

_____

_____

2. Choose one of the character traits of excellent employees. Write a short workplace scenario in which that virtue is either promoted or violated. Use an actual situation if you know of one. If not, make one up.

_____

_____

_____

_____

Thinking Critically

1. Apply the ETHICS model to Zeke's dilemma.

Zeke works for a large carpet-cleaning company. He and his partner, Estela, are dispatched by the company to businesses and residences. Zeke and Estela take a lot of pride in their work and professionalism. Customer evaluations score them very high in efficiency, quality of work, and courtesy. Even the pay is good. The problem is with their supervisor.

While Ms. Patterson treats Zeke well enough, she is consistently hostile and abusive toward Estela. The supervisor belittles and yells at Estela in front of other employees and customers. She has used words such as *stupid* and *useless* when talking about Estela to others. No matter what Estela does, she can't please Ms. Patterson.

Zeke considers Estela a friend, and it's hard for him to watch her being unfairly mistreated. He did try to talk with Ms. Patterson once about the issue, but she quickly turned her wrath on him. "This is between me and Estela," she warned. "Unless you want to get on my bad list, too, you'd better mind your own business."

Zeke is considering going over Ms. Patterson to report the matter to the vice president, but he isn't sure that would do any good. It certainly might make matters worse for him. Estela has talked many times about quitting, but she doesn't want to give Ms. Patterson the satisfaction.

What should Zeke do?

evaluate the problem: _____

_____

think through the options: _____

_____

_____

highlight the stakeholders: _____

_____

_____

identify and apply relevant ethical principles: _____

_____

_____

_____

_____

choose the wisest option: _____

_____

state your justification: _____

_____

_____

_____

2. Write a series of company policies that address one of the employee ethical misdeeds discussed in this chapter. Each policy should explain what behaviors are expected of employees, what behavior(s) will not be tolerated, and what the consequences are for violations of the policy.

_____

_____

_____

_____

Digging Deeper

1. Use newspapers, magazines, and online resources to find one example of workplace misconduct. Bring your example to class for discussion.

2. Find a corporate code of ethics by contacting businesses in your area or by researching corporate web sites. Highlight sections relevant to employee misdeeds or virtues discussed in this chapter.

3. Survey people at your school, looking for examples of employee misconduct. Ask people, "What is the worst thing you've ever seen an employee do at work?"

Personal Reflection

1. The most important ideas that I learned in this chapter were

2. This chapter made me think about

3. I would like to find out more about

4. One step that I could take to become a better employee is

11

Ethics and Corporate Responsibility

Chapter Goals

After completing this chapter, you should be able to:

- Identify a variety of corporate stakeholders and explain a company's obligations to each.

- Explain characteristics of socially responsible companies.

Key Terms & Concepts

stockholder model	retailer	stock
stakeholder model	supplier	philanthropy
turnover	distributor	
customer	wholesale price	

What do you think?

After graduating from college with a degree in business, Jerardo has an important decision to make. For whom is he going to work? One of the rewards of graduating with honors is that many companies granted him interviews. Several offered him entry-level management jobs. Two offers stood out above the others. Now Jerardo has to choose which one to accept.

While money is obviously a factor in his decision, Jerardo is mature enough to look beyond the first paycheck. Other factors include what cities he might have to move to, what opportunities he would have for advancement, and how well the business is managed. Social responsibility is also important to Jerardo because he grew up in a neighborhood that was neglected by local business and political leaders. Jerardo likes the idea of working for a company that gives something back to its community to help create a better place for everyone to live.

Company X has offered the highest starting salary, but it does not appear to have contributed much to improving community life or to helping charitable organizations. Company Y's salary offer is significantly lower, but the firm is well-known for its community programs, scholarships for local students, and donations to worthy causes. The two companies are about even with each other regarding the other issues that Jerardo thought were important.

It is tempting to go for the money. Jerardo tells himself that he could still contribute to charities and work to help others on his own. His efforts might even begin to transform Company X into a more socially responsible business. But it's a very big company, and he would be just one employee—a new one at that. It would be many years before Jerardo could make enough money to put much of a dent in the problems and needs of a community. Working for Company Y would mean a personal financial sacrifice, but he would be part of an organization committed to values that he shares.

Which offer should Jerardo accept?

You Decide

Read these short scenarios. Rate each one according to how serious an ethical concern you think the scenario represents. Circle the number on the scale. After each rating, write one sentence explaining why you rated the scenario as you did.

A. Company Blue produces a product that makes people's lives better, makes money for its stockholders, and provides jobs for thousands of employees. But the company cuts corners on environmental concerns and is causing a great deal of air and water pollution.

1	2	3	4	5
No ethical concern	Minor ethical concern	Moderate ethical concern	Important ethical concern	Very serious ethical concern

Explanation: _____

B. Company Green is a fast-food chain that keeps prices low by using produce picked by migrant workers who many people believe are exploited—forced to work long, hard hours for very low pay.

1	2	3	4	5
No ethical concern	Minor ethical concern	Moderate ethical concern	Important ethical concern	Very serious ethical concern

Explanation: _____

C. Company Gold produces makeup products that are tested on animals to ensure that the products are safe for humans. One test involves measuring how much of a product can be used before it causes blindness in an animal.

1	2	3	4	5
No ethical concern	Minor ethical concern	Moderate ethical concern	Important ethical concern	Very serious ethical concern

Explanation: _____

D. Company Red saves money by contracting out jobs to people in poorer nations who are willing to work for much less money than Americans are. The lives of the foreign workers are improved, but the unemployment rate in Company Red's community is steadily rising.

1	2	3	4	5
No ethical concern	Minor ethical concern	Moderate ethical concern	Important ethical concern	Very serious ethical concern

Explanation: _____

Corporate Obligations

The standard for measuring a company's success used to be simple. Now generally referred to as the **stockholder model**, the assumption was that a company's only important ethical obligation was to try to make as much money as possible for its investors and owners. How a company accomplished that was irrelevant. It might exploit its employees, as when young children used to be forced to work in dangerous coal mines. A business might save money by buying from suppliers that exploited their laborers, perhaps utilizing slave or prison labor. Or a corporation might save money by ignoring the fact that it was causing serious pollution, thereby endangering the communities around its plants and factories. As long as profits kept rolling in and the investors were happy, nothing else seemed to matter.

In the second half of the 20th century, attitudes began to change and evolve. The stockholder model was slowly replaced with a new way of thinking about corporate responsibilities—the **stakeholder model**. This view maintains that a company has legal and ethical responsibilities to its stakeholders, everyone affected by the decisions and actions of the business. Certainly, investors are affected, and their interests should be considered. But they are not the only people who should be considered. Others are affected, too—employees, suppliers, distributors, consumers, community members, perhaps even competitors. The central theme of the stakeholder model is that businesses should consider all of those various interests when making corporate decisions and plans.

> "He that is of the opinion money will do everything may well be suspected of doing everything for money."
>
> —Benjamin Franklin

Employees

How a business treats its employees tells much about the values and character of those who run the company. Some employers treat employees as little more than tools to be used up, discarded, and replaced. Some employees have to work in atmospheres that verge on corporate paranoia, with supervisors scrutinizing every action for imperfections and every statement for signs of disloyalty. While such administrators probably believe that those management styles are justified, the immediate and long-term consequences for the company can be disastrous.

Not surprisingly, when companies treat their employees badly, the morale of workers suffers. Employees feel used, victimized, and exploited. They do not experience pride in their company or fulfillment in their jobs. When those attitudes become pervasive, employee turnover becomes an expensive problem. **Turnover** refers to the number of employees a business is required to hire to replace workers who have left the company. Recruiting, interviewing, hiring, and training new employees can be a very expensive process, especially when large numbers of employees are leaving the company regularly. Fortunately, many business leaders understand that paying employees well and treating them with respect do save money in the long run.

Customers

A company that ignores its customers will not be in business for long. Customers provide the income necessary for companies to pay expenses and make a profit. Pleasing customers and keeping them satisfied should be a top priority for every business, and that is true for most companies. Most medium- to large-size companies employ customer relations specialists to appease the concerns and frustrations of buyers. Many offer special phone lines and e-mail addresses where customers can report their problems and have them resolved. For the majority of companies, keeping customers satisfied is a top concern. The customer is (almost) always right.

But some people in the business world view customers as objects to be exploited. Blinded by short-term thinking, these businesspeople deceive and manipulate customers to make quick sales. And because there are always people who can be deceived, these companies make sales that they may interpret as success. But left in their wake are many unhappy customers who come to realize that they were fooled and cheated. Many of them will tell their friends about the unethical company. Some may threaten, even follow through with, lawsuits. But none of them will be repeat customers, the lifeblood of most businesses.

It is not always easy to determine what constitutes a customer. Technically speaking, a **customer** is someone who buys a good or service. People usually think of a customer in terms of a **retailer**, a business that sells products directly to the general public. However, a company that manufactures plastic might sell most of its product to other companies. Those companies then use the plastic to make other products to sell to other businesses that distribute the products to retailers who sell the plastic products to people. The manufacturing company would need to consider all of those layers of businesses and people as customers.

Suppliers and Distributors

This layering effect in business occurs because most companies have suppliers and many utilize distributors. A **supplier** is a business that provides a particular service or commodity that other businesses require. The plastics manufacturer requires various chemicals and machines to make its product. It purchases those chemicals and machines from a number of different suppliers.

A **distributor** is a company that sells to retailers a product manufactured by others. The distributor purchases the product at a **wholesale price**, a discount offered when a customer buys goods in large quantities for the purpose of reselling them to others. For example, a company that makes cat food dishes does not usually sell them in its own stores. Instead, it sells them in large quantities to other businesses that distribute the products to retail stores that in turn, sell the dishes to cat owners.

There are many ethical concerns in the relationships among businesses, suppliers, distributors, and retailers. Since companies that buy from other companies fall into the role of customers, the same customer service issues of honesty and fairness apply. Suppliers sometimes sell inferior products to businesses or sell products at unfair prices. And sometimes businesses do not pay their suppliers in a fair and timely manner. Those practices are not especially wise in the long term. The offended businesses will likely find more honorable trading partners, and the poor reputation of the offending company will probably spread.

Communities

Perhaps the most ambiguous stakeholder relationships are between companies and the communities in which they build their factories and office buildings. After all, many members of the community may never buy or sell a single product or conduct business of any kind with a specific company in their town. Some citizens may not even realize that a particular company exists. Thus, they are little more than fellow citizens who live in the same area—neighbors, perhaps, but not much more.

Do people have legal or ethical obligations to their neighbors? Absolutely. You have a legal and ethical obligation not to steal from your neighbors or not to intentionally cause them harm. Many would argue that you have an ethical obligation to be a good neighbor. Similarly, businesses have legal and ethical obligations not to harm the citizens of their communities—and perhaps an ethical obligation to be a good neighbor, too.

There are many ways in which companies can harm members of the community. Polluting the air and water around factories can cause illness and death. Improperly storing, transporting, or disposing of dangerous chemicals can cause serious harm to people. Companies are held legally liable for damages that individuals suffer from those types of careless actions.

What makes a business a good neighbor? Generally, the same sorts of things that make people good neighbors. Businesses can be good neighbors by showing consideration for the needs and interests of the community, by taking leadership roles in helping to resolve community problems, and by sharing some of their wealth with community members who need help. Many companies understand that responsibility and invest time and money into improving the quality of life in their communities. The positive public relations that they receive in return often leads to higher employee morale and productivity and may attract additional business from the community.

Ethics & Law

Businesses have obligations not to damage the environment, and many federal laws require environmental responsibility. Those laws are sometimes violated. The Environmental Protection Agency (EPA) is the division of the federal government charged with enforcing environmental laws. The EPA maintains a web site that individuals and companies can use as a resource to help learn about and understand environmental laws. Explore the web site and find one interesting fact or resource to share with the class.

Stockholders and Investors

Stock is a financial instrument whose sale is used to raise capital for a corporation. As stated earlier, the stockholder model holds that the only important obligation of a business is to make money for those who own shares of stock in the company. In contrast, the stakeholder model maintains that a company has obligations to everyone affected by its decisions and actions. But a company's stakeholder group includes the stockholders who wager their money on the business's success. Companies have a legal and ethical obligation to try to produce a profit for their investors. However, that is not all that a company owes to those who invest in it.

Several recent corporate scandals have revolved around the fact that company administrators were less than honest with investors about the financial status of the business. To protect their jobs or the value of their own stock holdings, the executives misled investors into believing that the company was in much better financial shape than it actually was. Based on that information, some investors held on to stock that they otherwise might have sold or they bought additional shares. When the truth of the company's financial weakness came out, those investors lost far more money than they would have if the administrators had been honest with them.

Those deceptions constitute stock fraud and are a crime. Some of the corporate executives who acted dishonestly have been convicted and were forced to pay expensive fines and/or go to prison. A company does not have an obligation to make a profit for its investors, only to make a good faith effort to do so. But every business has an obligation to be honest with its investors, who are demonstrating their own good faith in the company by entrusting the business with their money.

"The leader who exercises power with honor will work from the inside out, starting with himself."

—Blaine Lee

Checkpoint

Briefly explain each of the following concepts.

stockholder model _____

_____

stakeholder model _____

_____

turnover _____

_____

customer _____

_____

retailer _____

_____

supplier _____

_____

distributor _____

_____

wholesale price _____

_____

stock _____

_____

What do you think now?

Reread the scenario at the beginning of the chapter, putting yourself in Jerardo's shoes. Would you choose to work for Company X or Company Y? Explain your reasons.

_____

_____

_____

Personal Reflection

Take another look at the list of factors that you decided would be important to you as you evaluated potential employers in the Personal Reflection on page 203. Rank-order the factors in terms of their importance to you. Start with the least important—the one that you would be willing to give up first—and write that factor on the first line. Then select the next least important, and so on, until you have all of the factors listed from least to most important.

What does your list say about your values, the things that matter most to you? How do you feel about that?

Characteristics of Socially Responsible Companies

Clearly, businesses have legal and ethical responsibilities to a variety of stakeholder groups. Identifying those responsibilities as obligations implies that they represent a sort of minimum standard. It is expected that all companies should fulfill the obligations. Businesses that do not are doing something wrong. What, then, sets apart those companies that go far beyond the minimum requirements by committing themselves to being good neighbors and good corporate citizens? What are the hallmarks of socially responsible companies?

Consideration for a Broad Range of Stakeholders

In 1982, seven people in the Chicago area died suddenly and mysteriously. Medical examiners concluded that each had swallowed a Tylenol capsule filled with cyanide. As newscasters spread the word of the murders, a national panic ensued. Investigators quickly concluded that the illegal tampering could not have occurred at the factory because the poisoned pills were from different lots that could have been shipped anywhere. Yet all of the poisonings occurred around Chicago. Someone in the Chicago area was tampering with the capsules and putting them back on the shelves. Could poisoned capsules be sitting on store shelves elsewhere in the country?

Johnson & Johnson, the maker of Tylenol, was faced with a nightmare. Although there was no evidence that anyone in the company had done anything wrong, the poisonings were threatening to ruin its business. In general, business experts acknowledged that Johnson & Johnson would never be able to sell another pill under the name of Tylenol. However, instead of trying to protect and defend the company's image, corporate executives decided to do whatever was necessary to protect the public. Johnson & Johnson immediately launched a national campaign at its own expense, warning people not to consume Tylenol until the extent of the poisonings was clear. The company issued the first national product recall, at a cost of $100 million, to pull every bottle of the medication off of every store shelf in the country. The company invented tamper-proof packaging and the one-piece caplet to make tampering virtually impossible. Johnson & Johnson offered a $100,000 reward for anyone who could identify the killer.

No corporation had ever gone to such lengths, far beyond any legal requirements, to protect the public from something that was not its fault. The extraordinary actions of the Johnson & Johnson administrators set a new standard for corporate social responsibility that is still held up as a role model in business schools today. When the company's president was later asked what guided the leaders to make the decisions that they did, he stated that they simply followed their company's statement of principles, The Johnson & Johnson *Credo*.

"Perpetual optimism is a force multiplier."

—Colin Powell

The Johnson & Johnson *Credo*

We believe our first responsibility is to the doctors, nurses and patients, to mothers and fathers and all others who use our products and services. In meeting their needs everything we do must be of high quality. We must constantly strive to reduce our costs in order to maintain reasonable prices. Customers' orders must be serviced promptly and accurately. Our suppliers and distributors must have an opportunity to make a fair profit.

We are responsible to our employees, the men and women who work with us throughout the world. Everyone must be considered as an individual. We must respect their dignity and recognize their merit. They must have a sense of security in their jobs. Compensation must be fair and adequate, and working conditions clean, orderly and safe. We must be mindful of ways to help our employees fulfill their family responsibilities. Employees must feel free to make suggestions and complaints. There must be equal opportunity for employment, development and advancement for those qualified. We must provide competent management, and their actions must be just and ethical.

We are responsible to the communities in which we live and work and to the world community as well. We must be good citizens—support good works and charities and bear our fair share of taxes. We must encourage civic improvements and better health and education. We must maintain in good order the property we are privileged to use, protecting the environment and natural resources.

Our final responsibility is to our stockholders. Business must make a sound profit. We must experiment with new ideas. Research must be carried on, innovative programs developed and mistakes paid for. New equipment must be purchased, new facilities provided and new products launched. Reserves must be created to provide for adverse times. When we operate according to these principles, the stockholders should realize a fair return.

Reprinted courtesy of Johnson & Johnson.

Note how many different stakeholder groups are identified in the *Credo*. Yet it is clear that the company's first priority is to its customers, and that fact guided corporate leaders through the disaster. Far from being forever ruined as a product name, after less than five months, Tylenol products reclaimed the same market share as before the poisonings.

One characteristic of a socially responsible company is the ability to acknowledge the business's obligations to all of its various stakeholder groups and to prioritize those groups when necessary. Companies that care only about pleasing investors and stockholders tend to become obsessed with the bottom line. That obsession can lead to short-term thinking and unethical actions.

Concern for the Environment

Another trait of a socially responsible company is a sincere dedication to protect and preserve the environment. There is a sense in which this concern is tied to obligations to stakeholders. After all, employees, community members, and consumers can all be affected by environmental issues. But this commitment to the natural world can go beyond considering effects on stakeholder groups. In effect, the environment becomes another stakeholder and is protected for its own sake.

While some in the business world clearly favor profit over environmentalism, many corporate leaders have demonstrated that the two can go together—that good environmental policies can lead to higher profits and greater corporate success. It just requires a little creativity.

In 1987, a former British schoolteacher, Anita Roddick, decided to open a small cosmetic store next to a funeral parlor in Brighton, England. She gave it a simple name—The Body Shop. Her commitment to social justice and animal rights issues quickly set her business apart, and it grew rapidly. In an industry in which the norm was to test products on animals, Roddick took a principled and very risky stand. She declared that her stores would never sell any products that had been tested on animals. In addition, Roddick established a strong recycling program and created corporate policies to promote environmentalism and social justice. Her business grew to become one of the largest chains of cosmetics stores in the world. Roddick became the second wealthiest woman in England, behind only the Queen, and was presented with the Global 500 Environmental Award by the United Nations.

In 1978, long-time friends Ben Cohen and Jerry Greenfield took a college class on ice-cream making. Shortly thereafter, they decided to open an ice-cream shop and committed themselves to establishing an ethically principled business. Ben & Jerry's quickly became known for its creative flavors with quirky names and for a corporate dedication to protecting the environment. The two founders established strong, creative environmental policies and rewarded bonuses and promotions to those employees who suggested creative environmental ideas. The revolutionary company grew quickly and became one of the best-known ice-cream companies in the nation. The two friends eventually sold the company as multimillionaires.

Obviously, not all businesses with strong environmental policies will achieve the success of The Body Shop or Ben & Jerry's. But success is not usually the reason why companies establish policies to protect the natural world. Business leaders, like most people, realize that safeguarding the environment is in everyone's best interests. It's the right thing to do whether or not it pays off in huge profits.

Commitment to Give Something Back

A third characteristic of socially responsible companies is a sincere commitment to give something back to the communities that support their business. Many corporate leaders understand that the profits their companies make can create unique opportunities to improve the quality of life for others and to help people in need. The efforts to improve the well-being of others through charitable donations are referred to as **philanthropy**.

Examples of corporate philanthropy are everywhere. A local plumbing company sponsors a youth soccer team. The area McDonald's restaurants coordinate

Learn More

Use the Internet to explore corporate web sites, looking for examples of corporate philanthropic programs. Bring one example to class for discussion.

their efforts to sponsor a Ronald McDonald House to help the families of sick and injured children. A local attorney donates money each year to provide scholarships for graduating seniors. A restaurant donates extra food at the end of every business day to a local shelter. A large corporation in the area underwrites a theater that presents plays and concerts. A local shopping mall gives holiday presents to underprivileged children.

On the surface, those acts of generosity seem inconsistent with the purpose of business. If companies exist primarily to make money, why give a sizeable portion of it away? Cynics may assume that the efforts are profit-driven. After all, good public relations are good for the bottom line. While public relations may sometimes be a factor behind philanthropic acts, there are deeper and better motivations. Business leaders and employees have a natural desire to be proud of their companies. When employees see the corporation doing good things in the community, their morale improves. In addition, most people have experienced the good feelings that come from doing good deeds for others. Helping others can be its own reward. Coordinating charitable efforts with coworkers and colleagues creates opportunities to help far more people than most individuals can help on their own.

Checkpoint

Explain these characteristics of socially responsible corporations.

consideration for a broad range of stakeholders _____

_____

concern for the environment _____

_____

commitment to give something back _____

_____

What do you think now?

Recall the scenario from the beginning of the chapter. Certainly Company X has no legal obligation to improve the quality of the community or donate money to charitable organizations. Suppose that the leaders of the firm argued that the primary purpose of their business was to make money, not to make the world a better place. How would you respond? Would they be wrong? unethical? short-sighted? Explain your answer.

_____

_____

_____

Personal Reflection

Describe a time when you were personally philanthropic, volunteering with a charitable organization or going out of your way to help someone else. How did the experience make you feel about yourself?

Summary

Businesses have obligations to a variety of groups that are affected by the companies' actions and decisions. These stakeholder groups include employees, customers, suppliers, distributors, and the communities in which the companies are located.

Socially responsible companies go well beyond their minimal obligations to stakeholder groups. Characteristics of socially responsible companies include consideration for the interests of a wide range of stakeholder groups, a sincere concern for the environment, and a dedication to giving something back to the communities that support the businesses.

Vocabulary Builder

Match the following terms to their definitions:

1. _____ The assumption in business that a company's only important ethical obligation is to try to make as much money as possible for its investors and owners
2. _____ The assumption in business that a company has legal and ethical responsibilities to its stakeholders, everyone affected by the decisions and actions of the business
3. _____ A business that provides a particular service or commodity that other businesses require
4. _____ A business that sells to retailers a product manufactured by others
5. _____ A business that sells products directly to the general public
6. _____ A discount offered when a customer buys goods in large quantities for the purpose of reselling them to others
7. _____ Efforts to improve the well-being of others through charitable donations
8. _____ The number of employees a business is required to hire in order to replace workers who have left the company.
9. _____ Someone who buys a good or service
10. _____ A financial instrument whose sale is used to raise capital for a corporation.

a. customer
b. distributor
c. philanthropy
d. retailer
e. stakeholder model
f. stock
g. stockholder model
h. supplier
i. turnover
j. wholesale price

Reinforcement

1. Create a sample business. Write your own company credo, identifying your stakeholders and detailing the specific obligations that you have to each group.

_____

_____

_____

_____

2. Assume that you are an administrator for a medium- to large-size business. Your company has decided to become more socially responsible by investing money into programs that will improve the quality of life for people in your community. You have been placed in charge of the Social Responsibility Project. In a paragraph, explain one program that you would recommend, how it would work, whom it would help, and how it would benefit the community as a whole.

_____

_____

_____

_____

Thinking Critically

1. Apply the ETHICS model to Teresca's dilemma.

Teresca is a new quality control specialist for a company that manufactures carpets and rugs. Since the manufacturing process involves using a variety of toxic chemicals, one of her jobs is to monitor the environmental effects of the factory on the surrounding area. She spends her days taking measurements of air and water quality in and around the community. Her reports are reviewed by supervisors and then sent on to government agencies. After a few months on the job, she begins to understand how the company wants the system to work.

When Teresca's measurements indicate that the air and/or water qualities are poor, she is assigned to long, hard hours of work to repeat her measurements until the data falls within acceptable ranges. When her measurements show good or excellent environmental conditions, her supervisors give her time off with pay and small congratulatory gifts. This week for the first time, Teresca intentionally adjusts the numbers a little. The water quality is only a few points under the acceptable standard, but she is tired and wants to go home. She raises the number so it falls within the range, turns in her reports, and clocks out.

Teresca feels very guilty that night and the next morning. She has falsified data on a government report, a federal crime. She decides to confess what she has done to her manager. But when Teresca arrives at work, she finds flowers on her desk from the management team, along with a $500 bonus check! When she mumbles to her supervisor that she doesn't think she deserves it, he replies, "Nonsense! You're doing a great job here. We appreciate your hard work and dedication to the company." Under his breath he adds, "And we really appreciate it when employees go out on a limb to protect the company."

Teresca now understands what the job will entail. The company does not view her job as one of measuring data, but of managing data to keep the business out of trouble with the government. She feels trapped. She moved across the country to get this job, using all of her savings in the process. She does not have family to fall back on for help. If she quits, she has nowhere to go and no guarantee that anyone else will hire her.

What should Teresca do?

evaluate the problem: _____

_____

think through the options: _____

_____

_____

highlight the stakeholders: _____

_____

_____

identify and apply relevant ethical principles: _____

_____

_____

_____

_____

choose the wisest option: _____

_____

state your justification: _____

_____

_____

_____

2. Sometimes businesses face situations in which the interests of stakeholders are in conflict. To do what is best for employees or customers might harm the interests of investors. Producing a maximum return for investors could mean cutting salaries or raising prices. How do you think companies should resolve such conflicts? How should the stakeholder groups be prioritized?

_____

_____

_____

_____

Digging Deeper

1. Find a business in your area that participates in some form of philanthropy. Interview someone at the company, learning more about what the company does, why the company does it, and what benefits the programs bring to the company.

2. Conduct a phone or e-mail interview with a representative of a charitable organization or social service agency. Briefly explain the theme of this chapter and ask for information about how businesses in the area help support the goals and programs of the organization.

3. Conduct research about an environmental problem in your area. Which businesses, if any, are involved? How? What is being done to resolve the problem?

Personal Reflection

1. The most important ideas that I learned in this chapter were

2. This chapter made me think about

3. I would like to find out more about

4. One step that I could take to be more socially responsible in my community is

advertising the practice of attracting public attention to a product or business for the purpose of increasing sales (p. 100)

affirmative action a policy that seeks to adjust past discrimination through active measures to ensure equal opportunity (p. 169)

audit the examination of financial records or accounts to check their accuracy (p. 132)

authority a source of ethical beliefs holding that an action is right or wrong because "someone important said so" (p. 12)

bait and switch the illegal practice of advertising a product at a low price and supplying only a limited quantity so customers may be lured into buying similar, but more expensive items that are in stock (p. 102)

benefit in business, an inducement above and beyond a wage or salary that employers offer to employees (p. 175)

boycott to refrain from using, buying, or dealing with a company or product as an act of protest (p. 176)

caring looking out for the interests of someone or something; the basis for Gilligan's Model of Moral Development (p. 63)

churning the unethical practice of encouraging investors to make multiple unnecessary trades in order to create extra income for a broker (p. 134)

class-action lawsuit a lawsuit in which one party or a limited number of parties sue on behalf of a larger group to which the parties belong (p. 119)

code of ethics a written set of principles or rules intended to serve as a guideline for ethical behavior, usually for the members of a group or an organization (p. 105)

collective bargaining negotiations between organized workers (trade unions) and employers to pressure companies into paying higher wages and offering more and better employee benefits (p. 176)

commission a fee or percentage of sales given to a salesperson based on the quantity of items or services sold in addition to regular wages (p. 119)

computer virus a computer program designed to replicate itself by copying itself into the other programs stored in a computer; it can be spread when information is shared between computer systems; it may cause a program to operate incorrectly, or it may corrupt a computer's memory (p. 153)

conflict of interest a conflict between one's private interests and public obligations (p. 119)

consequences the effects or results of what people do (p. 27)

copyright the legal right granted to an author, a composer, a playwright, a publisher, or a distributor to exclusive publication, production, sale, or distribution of a literary, musical, dramatic, or artistic work (p. 152)

credit report a detailed report of an individual's credit history prepared by a credit bureau and used by a lender to help determine a loan applicant's creditworthiness (p. 133)

critical thinking the process of logical problem solving (p. 78)

cronyism the practice of showing workplace favoritism toward one's friends (p. 170)

culture a source of ethical beliefs holding that the morality of an action depends on the beliefs of one's culture or nation (p. 12)

customer any person or entity that buys a good or service (p. 204)

discrimination the illegal treatment of a person or group based on a prejudice regarding race, gender, age, religious beliefs, ethnic origin, marital status, or disability (p. 169)

distributor a business that sells to retailers a product manufactured by other suppliers (p. 204)

diversity in business, the practice of recruiting, hiring, including, and incorporating people of all types and backgrounds throughout a company (p. 169)

duty an ethical obligation that one individual has to others (p. 33)

egoism principle the idea that the right thing for a person to do in any situation is the action that best serves that person's long-term interests (p. 28)

either/or a fallacy based on making it appear that there are only two possible sides to an issue, one good and one bad (p. 80)

ethical character possessing the personal courage and self-discipline to follow through and do what is right in situations of great temptation or pressure (p. 52)

ethical issues topics or actions that raise questions of right or wrong (p. 6)

ethical judgment the ability to determine the morally right or best course of action (p. 51)

ethical motivation the inner desire to do the right thing, to be a good person (p. 51)

ethical principles general guidelines for how people should or should not act (p. 5)

ethics the subfield of philosophy that studies the morality of human conduct; what is considered right or wrong, good or bad (p. 6)

ETHICS model a six-step structured approach to making ethical decisions where the goal is to determine the wisest and most ethical course of action (p. 86)

false advertising an advertising practice that makes statements about products the advertiser knows are not true (p. 101)

false appeal to authority a fallacy based on incorrectly relying on authority figures or experts to support an argument (p. 83)

false appeal to popularity a fallacy based on assuming that an idea is right because many people believe it is right (p. 83)

false prizes a sales technique that tricks potential customers into thinking they have won valuable gifts or prizes (p. 118)

favoritism a form of discrimination based on partiality toward a favored person or group (p. 170)

fear of change the inner force that holds people back from personal growth, which keeps them where they are (p. 67)

fiduciary obligation the responsibility of a financial professional to act in the best interest of the client (p. 134)

finance the management of money, banking, investments, and other assets (p. 131)

fraud deliberately deceiving someone in order to secure an unlawful or unfair gain (p. 123)

Golden Mean the method of defining virtues as perfect balances between opposite and undesirable extremes (p. 37)

guarantee an assurance attesting to the durability or quality of a service or product (p. 107)

hacking the act of illegally using computer equipment to "break into" the computer systems of others (p. 153)

hasty generalization a fallacy based on assuming that most members of a group share a common characteristic when the assumption is actually based on only a few observations (p. 81)

honesty the quality of being truthful (p. 191)

hostile environment a form of harassment in which supervisors or coworkers use embarrassment, humiliation, or fear to create a negative climate that interferes with a person's ability to perform his or her job (p. 171)

human resources the department in a company or corporation that is responsible for personnel recruitment, hiring, and management (p. 169)

identity theft stealing another person's personal information, such as credit card account numbers and Social Security numbers, to use as one's own for personal financial gain (p. 151)

inconsistency a fallacy based on contradicting oneself in words or actions without being able to logically defend the contradictions (p. 80)

industrious diligent in work or study; skillful, clever (p. 192)

inner conflict the inner force that motivates people to move up toward higher levels of ethical thinking (p. 66)

insider trading the illegal practice of buying or selling shares of stock or other investments on the basis of information that is not available to the public (p. 134)

integrity the adherence to a strict moral and ethical code (p. 191)

intuition a source of ethical beliefs holding that right and wrong have been built into a person's conscience and that he or she will know what is right by listening to that "little voice" within (p. 12)

is/ought a fallacy based on the fact that because things are a certain way now, they should remain that way (p. 81)

justice impartial fairness, equity; the basis for Kohlberg's Model of Moral Development (p. 54)

justification the arguments that support a decision (p. 90)

legalism the belief that because there are laws and policies to cover issues of right and wrong, ethics is irrelevant (p. 7)

logical fallacies illogical or deceptive arguments (p. 79)

loyalty a faithful allegiance to a person, an organization, a cause, or an idea (p. 192)

moral development the process of growing more ethically mature (p. 54)

moral sensitivity the ability to recognize and identify ethical issues, questions, and temptations (p. 50)

morality the part of human conduct that can be evaluated in terms of right and wrong (p. 6)

nepotism the practice of granting workplace favoritism to one's relatives (p. 170)

obligation a duty that one person has to another person (p. 175)

outsourcing the practice of contracting work to people and companies outside of one's own company or country (p. 176)

philanthropy the effort to increase the well-being of others through charitable aid or donations (p. 210)

phishing scams unethical attempts to attain someone else's personal financial information using phone calls, the mail, or the Internet (p. 151)

piracy the unauthorized and illegal reproduction, sale, distribution, or other use of a copyrighted work (p. 152)

plagiarism the act of taking work written or created by someone else and using it as one's own (p. 157)

post hoc a fallacy based on assuming that because two events happened in a short period of time, the first action must have caused the second action (p. 81)

price gouging the practice of pricing a product far above the normal market value on the basis that consumers have no other way to buy the product (p. 118)

principle of duties the idea that people should do what is ethically right purely because they have a moral obligation to do what is ethically right (p. 34)

principle of rights the idea that an action is considered moral when it respects the rights of others; it is considered immoral when it violates another's rights (p. 31)

principle of virtues the idea that ethics is based on being a good person, on incorporating ideal character traits into one's life (p. 36)

provincialism a fallacy based on looking at an issue from your own point of view or from the point of view of people similar to you (p. 83)

puffery an advertising practice that uses statements that are not outright lies, but bold exaggerations (p. 102)

questionable claim a fallacy based on using statements that are too broad or too exaggerated to be true (p. 82)

quid pro quo a Latin phrase meaning "something for something else"; a form of harassment in which sexual demands are directly tied to a person keeping his or her job or receiving a promotion or another job benefit (p. 171)

reason a source of ethical beliefs holding that consistent, logical thinking should be the primary tool used in making ethical decisions (p. 12)

red herring a fallacy based on using an unrelated idea in an argument to distract your opponent (p. 81)

relativism the belief that because ethical beliefs vary so widely, there can be no universal ethical principles that apply to everyone (p. 7)

respect to feel or show consideration and appreciation for someone or something (p. 192)

respect for persons the idea that it is wrong to use other people in ways that harm them for one's own benefit (p. 34)

retailer a business that sells products directly to the general public (p. 204)

reverse discrimination the practice of giving jobs and promotions to less qualified minority applicants at the expense of better qualified members of majority groups (p. 170)

right a term used to describe how an individual is entitled to be treated by others (p. 31)

selling the practice of exchanging goods for money (p. 117)

sexual harassment a form of discrimination based on making unwanted and offensive sexual advances, remarks, or acts, especially by a supervisor, as a condition of employment or promotion (p. 171)

slippery slope a fallacy based on an attempt to frighten others into rejecting an idea by trying to show that accepting it would start a chain reaction of terrible events (p. 82)

social contract a higher moral authority that represents the deepest values and beliefs of a society (p. 58)

spam unsolicited electronic advertisements (p. 152)

stakeholder model the assumption in business that a company has legal and ethical responsibilities to its stakeholders (p. 203)

stakeholders people or groups of people who might be affected by a specific decision because the consequences may affect them (p. 88)

standard an accepted level of behavior to which people are expected to conform (p. 14)

standard of ethics social expectations of people's moral behavior (p. 16)

standard of etiquette social expectations concerning manners or social graces (p. 14)

standard of law rules of behavior imposed on people by governments (p. 15)

stock a financial instrument whose sale is used to raise capital for a corporation (p. 206)

stockholder model the assumption in business that a company's only important ethical obligation is to try to make as much money for its investors and owners as possible (p. 203)

straight commission the pay structure for a salesperson who receives no hourly wage or salary; it is based entirely on a percentage of the total amount sold (p. 119)

substantiation the validation of advertising claims supported by objective data from independent research (p. 106)

supplier a business that provides a particular service or commodity that other businesses require (p. 204)

telemarketing the practice of selling directly to individuals through unsolicited phone calls, e-mails, or faxes (p. 102)

testimonial an endorsement of a product by someone claiming to have benefited from its use (p. 107)

trouble-shooter a person hired in a corporation to solve specific problems (p. 188)

turnover the process of recruiting, hiring, and training new employees to replace others who have left the company (p. 204)

two-wrongs-make-a-right a fallacy based on defending a wrong act by pointing out that someone else committed the wrong act, too (p. 80)

universal ethical principles self-chosen beliefs and values that are shared by all rational-thinking people (p. 59)

universal principles guidelines that rational people thinking logically agree everyone should follow (p. 5)

universality the idea that people should act as they would want others to act in the same situation (p. 34)

usury the practice of lending money and charging the borrower an excessively high rate of interest (p. 133)

utility principle the idea that the morally right action is the one that produces the best consequences for everyone involved, not just for one individual (p. 28)

value system a way of viewing ethical right and wrong, often unique to an individual, a culture, or a subculture (p. 26)

virtue an ideal character trait that people should try to incorporate in their lives; a trait commonly found in ethically mature people (p. 36)

warranty a written promise to repair or replace a product if it breaks or becomes defective within a specified period of time (p. 107)

whistle-blowing the act of reporting unethical or illegal wrongdoing within an organization to the public or to those in positions of authority (p. 193)

wholesale price a discount price offered to a customer, usually when a large quantity of a product is purchased (p. 204)